German PzKpfw IV Ausf. F2 (foreground), Ausf. F1 and PzKpfw IIIs on the Eastern Front in the summer of 1942. (Bundesarchiv)

AGGRESSORS

VOLUME 1

TANK BUSTER
VS.
COMBAT VEHICLE

Text by ALEX VANAGS-BAGINSKIS

Illustrations by RIKYU WATANABE

Ju87G-1 of *Verschskommando für Panzerbekämpfung.* (Bundesarchiv)

The 40 mm cannon-armed Hawker Hurricane Mk IID of No. 6 Squadron, RAF at Shandur, Egypt, in 1942. (Imperial War Museum)

Acknowledgments

I would like to express my gratitude to all my friends and acquaintances who have helped me in the preparation of this book, particularly Alexander Boyd, Peter Chamberlain, Cristopher F. Foss, Roger A. Freeman, William S. Godden OBE, Ian V. Hogg, Hans E. Krüger and Martin Streetly. I would also like to acknowledge the valuable help received from the Public Office at Kew, London. To all I extend my most sincere thanks.

Alex Vanags-Baginskis

First published in the United States of America by Howell Press, Inc., 700 Harris Street, Suite B, Charlottesville, Virginia 22901.
Telephone (804) 977-4006.

Library of Congress Catalog Card Number 89-82171
ISBN 0-943231-31-0
Printed in Japan.
First printing
HOWELL PRESS

Introduction

The tank and the armed aircraft began their careers as military novelties in World War I but played an important part in its conclusion. While the aircraft was gradually evolved for various military roles, the tank was specially designed to break the deadly power of the machine gun and regain mobility on the battlefield. Less than a quarter of a century later, they were to meet in combat as fully fledged weapons in a contest that has not been resolved to this day.

The idea of using aircraft against tanks goes back to 1917 when successful attempts were made by individual German fighter pilots to stop British tanks by machine-gunning them from above, but for some reason this early 'tank killing' tactic was never used on an organised basis, and even the armoured

ground attack aircraft pioneered by the Germans remained tied to infantry support.

The conflict that rekindled this contest was the Spanish Civil War, where the two major Continental military powers and ideological opponents, Germany and the Soviet Union, tested their new weapons in combat, assessed their development potential, gained invaluable practical experience and evolved new tactics.

By autumn 1939 all the ingredients of the 'flying tank buster' story were present: the prototype Ilyushin *Shturmovik* and Henschel Hs129 armoured ground attack aircraft; the first modern large-calibre aircraft cannon; the first efficient aircraft rockets; and the first prototypes of the advanced T-34 battle tank.

The appearance of 'flying tank busters' had similar causes in the West and on the Eastern Front, differing only in detail and the scale of the conflict.

It arose from the contest between progressively better armed and protected tanks and anti-tank guns,

which could never be provided in sufficient numbers everywhere to meet the threat posed by the highly mobile armoured fighting vehicles. Various close-combat weapons were only an exigency measure, the obvious counter being the mobile anti-tank gun, which led to the very successful German and then Allied assault guns. Basically tanks without turrets, these new weapons also had the same inherent drawbacks, especially as regards mobility at short notice and a limited scope in action. A suitably armed aircraft seemed to be the best solution to all these problems, apart from taking advantage of the weaker, protected upper parts of tanks.

The first aircraft used specifically against armour were the Soviet *Shturmovik*s, which began using air-to-ground rockets in summer 1941. However, the first dedicated 'tank busters' were the British Hurricane IID fighter conversions armed with two 40 mm cannon, which achieved quite notable successes in North Africa in 1942. It was at this time that the increasing number of improved Soviet tanks began to overwhelm the German defences on the Eastern Front, leading to the introduction of the cannon-armed Hs129B and Ju87G 'flying tank busters'. With the appearance of the German Tiger and Panther tanks, the cannon-armed anti-tank aircraft lost favour in the West, giving way to the rocket-carrying Typhoon ground support fighter. The Americans had no special 'tank busters' as such, but the P-47 Thunderbolt proved a most powerful and rugged ground support aircraft. While a few units tried their hand with rocket armament, most P-47 pilots preferred to hunt their armoured prey with bombs, developing remarkable skills at swooping down in accurate dives.

The following pages present an account of how these 'flying tank busters' came into being on the opposing sides during World War II, their operational use, the tactics evolved, and the measure of successes they achieved.

Hawker Typhoon Mk IB (far above) and Republic P-47D Thunderbolt. Both planes carry 500 lb (227 kg) bombs under their wings.

The appearance of 'tank busters'

The Spanish Civil War has been rightly described as the testing ground for World War II. What began as an internal political conflict in July 1936 soon gained ideological and material support abroad and, to many people, became an emotional issue.

Two of the largest military powers in the world at that time took their sides, the Soviet Union and Germany, and not just for altruistic or ideological reasons either. It was a unique opportunity to try out some of their latest weapons in action, to test their military theories in practice, to learn and evolve new ideas, and for their specialist troops and commanders to gain combat experience in rotation.

The Spanish Civil War was also the first occasion modern military aircraft, armoured fighting vehicles and their opposing weapons met in combat in circumstances where their performance and effect could be readily observed and evaluated by opponents and neutrals alike.

Although to a large extent Spain is not a 'tank country' and the use of armoured fighting vehicles was limited, there were encounters on both sides involving armour and anti-tank weapons which had an important bearing on future developments. The same applied to the use of air power and, more specifically, aircraft in close support operations.

The armoured equipment of the opposing sides was very unequal. The Republicans were supplied with a number of Soviet BT-5 and BT-7 light/medium tanks, T-26B infantry support tanks and BA-10 armoured cars. All four were standard equipment of the Red Army, and most were armed with 45 mm cannon. On the Nationalist side, the only modern armoured fighting vehicles were the Italian CV 33 and CV 35 tankettes and German PzKw I light tanks—no match for any of the Soviet vehicles.

When the armour was first used during a Republican counterattack on the Jarama front in February 1937, it came as a profound shock to the Soviet observers: the German 37 mm Pak 35/36 anti-tank guns had no difficulty in overcoming the 16–25 mm armour of the T-26B at considerable distances, even at an angle.

Some months later, the first BT tanks used in action in Spain did not fare much better; their 13 to 20 mm armour offered even less protection. The main reason for this dismal performance was the misuse of these fast tanks in an infantry support role where their high-velocity 45 mm guns could not offset the relatively thin armour—a fact quickly recognised by Soviet observers.

These encounters on the Spanish terrain resulted in almost diametrically opposite conclusions. The German military believed their standard 37 mm anti-tank gun had no equal and that there was no real need for a larger-calibre weapon for some time. However, as a safeguard the Rheinmetall-Borsig concern were asked to start development work on a new 50 mm anti-tank gun in summer 1937 but without any urgency attached to it.

Soviet conclusions were not so complacent. It was obvious their tanks needed thicker armour and better armament. Just as important was their cross-country performance. What is more, everything learned in Spain first had to be translated into solutions best suited for the Russian terrain, which was quite different. In short, a new medium tank was essential.

The immediate result was the experimental 28-ton T-46-5 (or T-111) with 60 mm armour protection, designed to resist the German 37 mm anti-tank gun. Although still armed with the standard 45 mm tank gun, the T-46-5 was the first step that eventually led to the formidable T-34.

The origins of its stablemate, the sleek and powerful T-34, can be traced back to the earlier BT series of track/wheel tanks, developed via several experimental models with sloping armour to the novel diesel-powered A-32 of summer 1939, and finally the A-34, the immediate T-34 prototype.

After more combat lessons gained against the Japanese forces in the Far East in August 1939 and the first reverses in Finland confirmed the urgent need for better armour protection, the decision was made in December 1939 to standardise on just one type of medium (T-34) and one heavy support tank (KV-1). The first T-34 was completed at Kharkov in January 1940 and, after very thorough trials, ordered in large-scale production five months later. By that time, the first KV-1s were already undergoing service trials.

These new Soviet tanks were evolved in great secrecy

BT-7 medium tank. (Novosti Press)

T-26B infantry support tank. (Novosti Press)

and, thanks to the efficiency of Soviet Intelligence, with full confidence that no existing anti-tank gun or tank could harm them in straight combat. In June 1941, exactly a year later, the T-34 and KV-1 came as an unpleasant surprise to the German troops and command alike, whose still standard 37 mm anti-tank guns proved useless. By summer 1942 the growing number of T-34 tanks constituted a menace and led directly to the creation of the first German 'flying tank busters'.

Less glamorous but in many ways more important to the outcome of battles was the work of aircraft used in close support and ground attack roles. The only activities that have received some publicity were ground attacks flown by the obsolete German He51 biplanes after they had proved inferior to Soviet-built fighters.

In fact, the first large-scale use of aircraft against ground targets, including armour, took place during the battle of Guadalajara on 8 March 1937, when more than 100 Republican R-Z biplanes, I-15 bis and I-16 fighters relentlessly attacked a strong Italian force, including over 60 light tanks, advancing towards Madrid. Two days later the disorganised Italian troops were struck and routed by counterattacking Republican ground forces.

Although not specifically a 'tank busting' action, a number of light Italian tanks were destroyed and damaged from the air, which did not escape the notice of Soviet observers.

Contrary to other countries, satisfied with light bombers and adapted reconnaissance aircraft, or experimenting with dive bombers, the Soviet military leadership envisioned a specially designed aircraft best suited for 'tank busting'. An obvious precondition was armour protection against ground fire, particularly machine guns, as a result of which all Soviet projects and designs of this class included varying amounts of armour plating.

It is quite possible that the armour-protected German ground support aircraft of 1917/18 had some influence on Soviet design: they were the only machines specially designed for use against ground targets and most successful in action. The most advanced were the Junkers designs, the J.I biplane and CL.I low-wing monoplane being the first all-metal military aircraft used on operations.

In any case, soon after the appearance of the first indigenous Soviet military aircraft came the *Shturmoviks*. Their development was encouraged by such important Soviet personalities as Tukhachevski, one of the most progressive of Red Army commanders, who foresaw the development of large-scale armoured warfare and who reiterated the urgent need for effective anti-tank aircraft.

In the early 1930s there were also protracted Soviet experiments with recoilless aircraft cannon of 76 to 102 mm calibre, in part specifically for anti-tank use, but none reached the series production stage. The initially very promising recoilless 76 mm APK-4 cannon was Stalin's favourite 'secret weapon' for almost five years, with vast sums of money and other resources allocated for its development. With all that, the Soviet engineers never solved the tendency of these weapons to suddenly jam and explode, as well as their lack of sufficient muzzle velocity for accurate air gunnery, so all further work was abandoned and the designer arrested in February 1936. After this expensive fiasco Stalin became deeply suspicious of all Soviet designers and engineers working on the more unconven-

tional aspects of military technology, which had a detrimental effect on all new weapons.

Nevertheless, the Soviets receive the credit for proposing the first 'flying tank buster' project as such from the outset.

Early in 1936, as part of the Soviet's modernisation programme, the Main Administration of the Soviet Air Force prepared a specification for an anti-tank aircraft and issued it to the design bureau led by Nikolai Polikarpov (then part of the TsKB, the Central Design Bureau group). Designated the TsKB-44, the new project was known as VIT-1 (*Vozdushny Istrebit'el Tankov*—Airborne Tank Destroyer), and work on it was completed in July 1936.

The original proposal called for a sleek, twin-engined two-seater with a single fin/rudder assembly, fitted with two exceptionally heavy 37 mm ShK cannon in its wing roots and two 20 mm ShKAS cannon in the fuselage nose. A variant projected after the first reports from Spain envisioned a forward-firing armament of no less than four 37 mm cannon.

In any event, the dedicated 'tank buster' project was not accepted, and on official request the design had to be altered to a three-seater with a twin fin/rudder assembly capable of fulfilling additional roles, as indicated by its parallel functional designations SVB (*Samolyot Vozdushnovo Boya*—Air Combat Aircraft) and MPI-1 (*Mnogomestny Pushechny Istrebit'el*—Multi-seat Cannon Fighter). The sole TsKB-44 built was an unarmed prototype powered by two 960 hp Klimov M-103 in-line engines, the most powerful then available. It was test-flown in summer 1937.

The following VIT-2 (TsKB-48) was basically similar but featured a redesigned fuselage incorporating a large fuel tank between the nose cabin and the radio operator/gunner. The only concession to its supposed anti-tank role was the retention of two 37 mm cannon in the wing roots. The unarmed VIT-2 prototype was first flown on 11 May 1938, but due to another change in official policy, influenced by the performance of the German Ju87 dive bombers in Spain, the aircraft began to be regarded as a potential twin-engined dive bomber. However, for various reasons the resulting SPB(D) never reached series production stage.

Although eventually not built as such, the VIT is of interest as the first purposely designed anti-tank aircraft and might have been developed as such if too much had not been demanded of it.

The changes in Soviet Air Force policy had a lot to do with operational reports from Spain and their translation to Russian terrain conditions. These resulted in the formulation in November 1937 of a new set of specifications for a modern, heavily armoured ground attack/support aircraft with anti-tank capability. These specifications led to the BSh (Armoured Assaulter) design and the unique Il-2 *Shturmovik* of World War II fame.

But the Soviet military was not alone in thinking along these lines: seven months earlier, similar conclusions had been reached by the *Luftwaffe* experts.

Ostensibly, the Ju87 Stuka was the main German trump card, and dive bombing was the answer to all their military prayers—or so it seemed. But there was another, less publicised side to the evaluation of air operations in Spain, which resulted in a decision that, except for some details, practically matched Soviet conclusions.

While the fighting in Spain was still in the early stages, the German RLM (State Air Ministry) prepared a specification for a small, armoured ground attack/support aircraft with emphasis on protection for the pilot (no rear defence being stipulated). The basic fixed armament was to consist of at least two 20 mm cannon and two rifle-calibre machine guns. In April 1937, this official requirement was issued to four German aircraft firms, and on 1 October 1937 the RLM awarded development contracts to Focke-Wulf and Henschel. Their proposals were allocated the RLM numbers Fw189C and Hs129. While the two-seat Fw189C was a modification of the basic reconnaissance aircraft, the Hs129 was a completely new design, and a single-seater.

Developed by *Dipl. Ing.* Friedrich Nicolaus, the Hs129 represented his solution to the demanding requirements: the smallest possible airframe, which enclosed the pilot in an armoured cockpit shell made of seam-welded, angled armour plates, giving it and the fuselage a triangular shape. The bullet-proof cockpit glazing consisted of small 75 mm-thick panels, resulting in very restricted vision. The first Hs129 was flown in April 1939, and despite poor performance and many other objections, the type was ordered into production by the RLM later that year.

While the original Hs129A series with Argus As410A engines proved underpowered and sluggish and was not accepted by the *Luftwaffe*, the redesigned Hs129B powered by two 700 hp Gnôme-Rhône 14M radials from captured French stocks was more successful. First flown in early summer 1941, this revised ground attack aircraft arrived just after the German forces on the Eastern Front had experienced their first massed Red Army counterattacks and they felt limited shock effect of facing the first T-34 tanks and armoured *Shturmovik* 'assaulters'. The need for a counterweapon was becoming urgent, and the Hs129B-1 production series was allocated the highest priority. The new version incorporated two important changes: in addition to its built-in armament it could carry a variety of weapons fitted according to operational requirements, and it was the first to feature a detachable underfuselage pannier with

a 30 mm high-velocity cannon, making it a potent 'flying tank killer'.

Although development of the new Soviet *Shturmovik* began later than its German counterpart, the Soviet efforts were spurred by a much greater sense of urgency, as evidenced by the earlier appearance of the BSh-2 (or Il-2) assaulter.

In December 1937 the new *Shturmovik* specifications were issued to several Soviet aircraft design offices, and a month later those led by Sergei Ilyushin (of TsKB) and Pavel Sukhoi (of TsAGI, the Central Aero and Hydrodynamic Institute) were instructed to proceed with their proposals. While the Sukhoi design was to be dogged for many months by the recurrent problems with its new and untried M-71 double-row radial engine—which, together with the exigencies of war, eventually left it standing—the competing TsKB-55 had a head start. Sergei Ilyushin had studied *Shturmovik* designs for some time and, already in 1935, begun experiments investigating the use of double-curvature armour as an integral stress-bearing part of the aircraft. This novel and promising idea was associated with many problems, especially fabrication and welding, most of which seemed resolved by late 1937, and work on the two-seat TsKB-55 began in January 1938.

However, there were more snags with the welding of the all-important armoured shell than expected, and the first TsKB-55 could not be flown until 30 December 1939. The flight tests were disappointing; the aircraft was underpowered for its weight and barely manoeuvrable in clean condition.

By that time strong Soviet air and ground forces, including armour, had been involved in a bitter, undeclared war against the Japanese in Outer Mongolia from May until August 1939, followed three months later by an unprovoked all-out attack on Finland. In both conflicts the lack of armoured ground support/attack aircraft was painfully evident, and the Soviet Air Force command drew up revised specifications for a longer-ranging aircraft of this type, the completion of which was now a matter of the greatest urgency.

By late 1939 another new weapon had appeared in the Soviet armoury—the first air-launched rocket projectiles. Originally intended as an anti-bomber weapon on recommendations

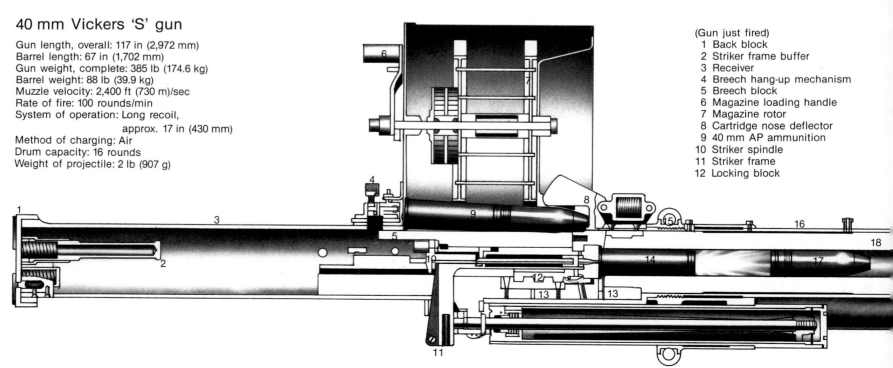

40 mm Vickers 'S' gun

Gun length, overall: 117 in (2,972 mm)
Barrel length: 67 in (1,702 mm)
Gun weight, complete: 385 lb (174.6 kg)
Barrel weight: 88 lb (39.9 kg)
Muzzle velocity: 2,400 ft (730 m)/sec
Rate of fire: 100 rounds/min
System of operation: Long recoil,
approx. 17 in (430 mm)
Method of charging: Air
Drum capacity: 16 rounds
Weight of projectile: 2 lb (907 g)

(Gun just fired)
1 Back block
2 Striker frame buffer
3 Receiver
4 Breech hang-up mechanism
5 Breech block
6 Magazine loading handle
7 Magazine rotor
8 Cartridge nose deflector
9 40 mm AP ammunition
10 Striker spindle
11 Striker frame
12 Locking block

of Soviet fighter pilots returned from Spain late in 1937, this novel weapon was temporarily delayed in its development by the arrest of the original group of Soviet engineers, and the finalised 82 mm RS-82 rockets were not air-fired until January 1939. Seven months later, the first RS-82s were tried out in combat against Japanese aircraft in Outer Mongolia but proved too cumbersome and inaccurate. However, their use against ground targets, including tanks, was another matter, and the RS-82 rockets were quickly adopted as optional armament for that purpose. (The same RS-82 rocket projectile was also adapted for ground use from multiple launchers, soon to be known as the 'Katyusha', the first of many.)

Due to the great urgency the revised Ilyushin ground attack aircraft, designated TsKB-57 or BSh-2 (Armoured Assaulter 2), featured practically the same airframe as its predecessor, except that to meet the longer range requirement and improve handling, the machine was now a single-seater, and the wing had been moved bodily forward by 60 cm (2 ft). Powered by a 1,600 hp Mikulin AM-38 engine, the prototype was first flown on 12 October 1940. State acceptance tests commenced on 28 February 1941 and were completed just one month later, by which time the new aircraft—now designated Il-2, but soon to be known worldwide as 'Shturmovik'—was already in production. The Soviet Air Force finally had its own flying 'tank buster'.

The German 'Blitzkrieg' tactics naturally had an effect on the British and American military planning as well, particularly as regards anti-tank measures.

The standard British anti-tank gun was the Ordnance 2-pounder (40 mm) which had performed reasonably well in France—where most of them had been left behind in June 1940. However, the anti-tank weapon was hard put to defeat the latest German PzKw III and IV tanks, whose guns also outranged it. Although the need for a more powerful anti-tank gun had been recognised in 1938, nothing like it was available in summer 1940, and production of the 40 mm weapon continued. It was the time of the expected German invasion of the British Isles and every gun was needed. Various other anti-tank measures were examined, tested and manufactured; of those only the PIAT rocket projector achieved service status.

But there was another defence against tanks: from the air.

Vickers-Armstrongs and Rolls-Royce began development of a new British 40 mm aircraft cannon in 1938. It was a time of feverish rearmament, and the first 40 mm Vickers gun was ready for prototype trials in August 1939. After successful functional tests the new weapon, now known as the Vickers 'S' gun, was put in limited production in spring 1940. By June 1940 the British Air Staff had decided against using large-calibre cannon in air combat and, prompted by events in France, initi-

Hurricane IID fitted with 'S' guns under the wings. (Imperial War Museum)

ated an enquiry regarding the use of aircraft cannon against tanks. The available 40 mm guns were the obvious choice, but for some reason it took more than six months before any urgency was attached to the idea. In fact, in spring 1941 a series of official tests was still carried out with 20 mm aircraft cannon, despite unsuitable ammunition and consistently poor results in trial shoots against derelict British tanks.

The first air firing tests with the Vickers 'S' gun took place in early 1941, and immediately afterwards 100 'S' guns were ordered from Vickers-Armstrongs, to be ready for delivery by August 1941. However, the arrival of German troops in North Africa, the superior performance of their medium tanks, and a lack of effective British anti-tank weapons soon changed the whole situation. The flying 'tank buster' had become an urgent necessity.

The only available modern single-engined British aircraft capable of carrying a pair of the new 40 mm cannon was the Hawker Hurricane, and the Air Ministry had informed Hawker Aircraft already in May 1941 of the Air Staff decision to use the Vickers 'S' guns against tanks. The situation in North Africa demanded urgent measures and no time could be lost. While suitable anti-tank ammunition was being developed by Vickers-Armstrongs, detailed modification drawings at Hawker's were completed in July, two Vickers 'S' guns received in August, and a Hurricane II fighter fitted with these weapons in streamlined fairings under the wings was first flown on 18 September 1941. Even before the firing tests were over, Hawker Aircraft received an order for the conversion of Hurricane II airframes with the strengthened wing; the new anti-tank version was designated the Hurricane IID.

Another, earlier underwing installation of the Vickers 'S' guns occurred on an RAF Mustang I Army cooperation fighter. Firing trials were very successful, but the Mustang was deemed unsuitable for service in the North African desert. In late 1941, large-calibre aircraft cannon were still in the experimental stage in the United States, and so the Hawker Hurricane IID was destined to become the first, and only, Western cannon-armed flying 'tank buster'.

13 Barrel extension	16 Barrel recoil cylinder	19 Barrel return springs
14 Cartridge case	17 Armor piercing shell	20 Barrel return springs tube
15 Trunnion block	18 Barrel	21 Muzzle fairing

Tank busters over the desert

Dispatched post-haste to help the retreating Italian ally stem the British advance into Libya, the first German troops landed in Tripoli on 14 February 1941. Two days later, a small motorised German unit made its first contact with some British troops near El Agheila and quickly knocked out three armoured cars without loss to themselves. General Erwin Rommel had arrived.

On 11 March three dozen German tanks were unloaded at Tripoli, and the newly created *Deutsche Africa Korps* (DAK) had gained its first armoured backbone. The rest is well known. General Rommel proved a master tactician, introducing the art of sudden armoured strikes and sidesteps, combined with quick reactions to any British moves, which helped him to preserve his generally numerically and materially inferior forces for the next two years and inflict serious losses to his opponents. But the German force in North Africa was limited by logistics: no more than four divisions could be kept supplied across the Mediterranean. Once the British had begun to understand the German Enigma machine code messages, which revealed German supply traffic, and take appropriate action, it was only a matter of time before the later German-Italian Panzer Army Africa would be caught short.

By late 1941 the armoured core of the DAK consisted of the 15 and 21 Panzer Divisions, with some light armour also used by the 90 Light Division; this situation was to remain unchanged until the Allied landing in Tunisia. In addition, there were several Italian armoured divisions equipped mainly with the 14-ton M.13/40 tanks and CV 35 tankettes. The German armour comprised a constantly changing number of PzKw III and IV medium tanks and PzKw II (and a few PzKw I) light tanks, supplemented by various captured British and American tanks. In early spring 1942 the first PzKw III Ausf. J tanks arrived in North Africa. This new version was armed with the long-barrel 50 mm L/60 gun and proved extremely useful in the desert, able to engage the British Valentine and Lend-Lease General Grant tanks with ease. But by far the best Axis tank in North Africa at that time was the PzKw IV Ausf. F2 armed with the 75 mm L/43 gun, which could outshoot any Allied tank extant in summer-autumn 1942. To the British, it was known as the Mk IV Special and was highly respected, but only a small number were ever shipped to the DAK.

By mid-1942 all German tanks carried additional armour plating bolted to their turrets and hull fronts, doubling the thickness of their standard armour protection—and the effort needed to knock them out.

Contrary to their German opponents who now had the very effective 50 mm Pak 38 anti-tank gun, augmented by some captured Soviet long-barrelled 76.2 mm Model 1936 field guns, which had been converted into very useful anti-tank guns—not to mention the superb 88 mm Flak 36 anti-aircraft gun used in anti-tank role—the British anti-tank gun situation in North Africa was grim. Their standard equipment was still the same 2-pounder (40 mm) anti-tank gun, long since outranged by German tank guns. In addition to using disabled tanks in a static role, an attempt was made to provide mobile anti-tank defences by mounting the 2-pounder gun on light trucks, facing backwards. Of course that did not improve its penetrating powers. The first 6-pounder (57 mm) anti-tank guns arrived in North Africa early in 1942, but their supplies were irregular, and there was never enough.

In spring 1942 the situation in North Africa had settled down to an uneasy calm. Both sides were building up their strengths. The British were led by General Auchinleck whose aim was 'destroying all German forces in the Gazala-Tobruk-Bir Hacheim area, followed by advance into Cyrenaica,' while the German-Italian forces were under nominal Italian supreme command but led in battle by General Rommel, who planned to attack and take Tobruk, a natural port and the second most important British base in North Africa.

During this interim period, No. 6 Squadron, RAF, which had served in the Middle East since 1919, was suddenly relieved of its few remaining aircraft. Orders received on 28 February 1942 indicated a re-equipment and a more offensive role for them in the immediate future. Two months later, No. 6 Sqn was just as suddenly transferred to Shandur in Egypt, where its pilots were introduced to their new mounts—the Hawker Hurricane IID armed with two 40 mm underwing cannon, the first specially evolved 'tank buster.'

Urgency was paramount, and the pilots immediately had to start low-level flight training. The following day, two armament experts from Britain began instructing the pilots and armourers in the use and maintenance of their new weapons—the Vickers 'S' guns. Everything had to be organised on the spot: cloth targets of gradually diminishing size stretched between two metal poles; practical advice on how to fly low without 'skimming' the sand dunes; and lessons on approaching

Five Hurricane IIDs preparing to take off from their desert airfield in North Africa in 1943. (Imperial War Museum)

the target at about 300 ft (90 m) altitude and then dipping down and flying towards it at about 20 ft (6 m) off the ground; not opening fire until about 150 yds (140 m) from the target; firing the guns in controlled 'pairs' (one round from each gun, fired together); and then getting away, using the terrain for cover before pulling up again.

On 12 May a captured German PzKw IV tank was towed to a nearby firing range, but before the pilots even had their first practice shoot urgent orders requested one Flight to be fully trained and ready for action by the end of the month. A few days later, some of the more experienced pilots gave a special demonstration shoot against the captured German tank, witnessed by several senior British tank and RAF officers from Cairo.

On 26 May Rommel pre-empted the planned British attack and opened his own offensive against the Gazala positions. While some Italian and German formations attacked the centre, the German armoured force, the 15 and 21 PzDivs and the 90 Light Division, had moved overnight to turn the southern flank of the Gazala line and then raced northwards, towards the sea—and Tobruk. But the southern gateway was blocked by the old desert fort of Bir Hacheim, held by 4,500 Free French troops under General Koenig, and the German advance was temporarily halted. No British tanks were anywhere near, and should Bir Hacheim fall, the German armour would be let loose behind the British lines.

This sudden development had an immediate effect on the budding 'tank buster' squadron. Instead of just one Flight as originally ordered, it now had to have two Flights ready for operations by the end of May, leaving the third Flight at Shandur, which was to become the permanent training base for 6 Sqn for several months. On 1 June the two Hurricane IID Flights were at Gambut, but after all that urgency nothing happened for a week. The first attempted attack on some reported German tanks was flown on 7 June but proved abortive; the armour could not be found.

The next day, three Hurricane IIDs led by Wing Commander Porteous, the squadron CO, were called out to attack some German armour west of Bir Hacheim, and this time they struck metal. On returning to base, the pilots claimed two unidentified tanks, one fuel pump and two trucks—the first vehicles destroyed by the 'flying tank busters'.

Although by then the DAK troops had grown used to low-level attacks by British fighter-bombers, they also knew from experience that the odd 20 mm cannon hit on armoured fighting vehicles seldom disabled them. Consequently, noticing another three Hurricanes approaching at low level, the German troops took cover as usual and were later surprised to discover that the expected machine gun damage had turned into something far heftier.

Unfortunately no eyewitness reports from the German side of this first 'tank buster' attack are available; it would seem the attacking aircraft were assumed to be ordinary Hurricane fighter-bombers.

The second operation that afternoon by another three Hurricane IIDs in the same area was not so successful: the ground defences were alerted, and one aircraft was shot down by Flak, while another pilot had to abandon his follow-up attack due to a stuttering engine. Even then, the two attacking Hurricane IIDs claimed one unidentified tank and two trucks destroyed. But this was hardly any relief for the French garrison at Bir Hacheim, and after some very bitter fighting, it had to be abandoned on the night of 11 June.

Two days later, five pilots of 6 Sqn were sent to attack some tanks south of El Adem, claiming one unidentified, two troop transports and one truck. A second operation the same afternoon was completely abortive—the reported tanks had disappeared.

Two vital lessons were learned that day. The morning raid had not produced the expected results because the enemy tanks were well dispersed among other vehicles, not worth the special armour-piercing ammunition. The afternoon raid was simply too late, indicating the need for the quickest possible communication of target reports; tanks were never stationary.

By then, the German armour was spreading out behind the Gazala positions, and 6 Sqn was forced to evacuate its base on 14 June, moving to LG 75 (Landing Ground) near 'Oxford Circus'—two arbitrary place names in the desert that cannot be found on any maps.

The day after came the first triple operation, this time against Axis armour already north of El Adem; the last attack was flown after 2000 hrs. The day's score amounted to 11 tanks and eight other vehicles hit in 11 sorties, at the cost of just one Hurricane IID hit by Flak. All except three of the tanks were identified according to type, and the pilots were careful to claim only hits, not destruction as before. It was also the first time the Vickers 'S' guns had failed: on two separate occasions they refused to fire during attacks. The early 40 mm ammunition

Hawker Hurricane Mk IID of the famous No. 6 Squadron flying over the Western Desert. (Imperial War Museum)

being used in the guns was soon discovered to be defective, and some rounds were missing propellant charges.

On 16 June, another eventful day, German armour was reported closing in around the 6 Sqn base but operations went ahead as ordered. During the two strikes flown that day the six pilots involved accounted for ten tanks and seven other vehicles, without any losses of their own. All these attacks were flown at very low level, and the Hurricane IID airplane piloted by Flt Lt Hillier actually hit the top of the PzKw III he was attacking, losing the tailwheel and half the rudder, but it managed to return to base.

A week later, the first batch of potential new 'tank buster' pilots arrived at Shandur: ten RAF Pilot Officers, comprising four Australians, three Britons, one New Zealander and two American volunteers.

During the two months beginning 22 June 1942, the start of Rommel's advance towards Egypt and the Suez Canal, there was much confusion, reflected in the activities of 6 Sqn, the only flying 'tank buster' unit in North Africa. Instead of making arrangements for fighter-reconnaissance patrols to keep track of Axis armour and radio their observations to a central coordinating HQ for an immediate decision on which of the reported armour should be attacked first, this unique formation seems to have been used haphazardly. In that period, 6 Sqn was called into action on just seven days, flying eleven operations, one of which was abortive; another did not find any targets. The score claimed for the total of 52 sorties was six German, 11 Italian and two unidentified tanks hit, as well as seven other armoured vehicles and guns, and 23 trucks. Losses amounted to three aircraft shot down by Flak and three lost in training accidents. It did not seem a good trade-off for just half a dozen German tanks, the principal target.

The situation on the ground was deteriorating rapidly. On 29 June German troops captured Mersa Matruch, taking over 6,000 prisoners—and that was just 300 km (90 mls) west of Alexandria. Two days later, the DAK made its first attempt to storm the El Alamein positions, the last defensive line before the Nile Delta, but that was as far as Rommel would get. His armoured formations were down to about 40 percent of their initial size, the troops were tired, and the badly needed supplies, now down to a trickle, moved along roads exposed to recurrent fighter-bomber attacks.

It was a different picture on the British side: despite reverses, their supplies were guaranteed, fresh armour and troops were arriving in increasing numbers, and reserves were being built up for the counterstroke. Their new commander was General Bernard Montgomery, who was determined not to risk his troops (or his own reputation) before he had the necessary superiority.

After the hectic June, the 'tank buster' squadron seems to have been held back in reserve, training and practising for the expected all-out German–Italian attack. Officially, the squadron intended to increase its complement to 28 pilots.

In an attempt to minimise losses due to ground defences, it was decided to introduce close fighter escort, which was to be combined with top cover whenever possible. This new tactic was first tried out in action on 1 September 1942. On that day, No. 7 SAAF (South African Air Force) Sqn as detailed for close escort, and three of its Hurricane II fighters, armed with light bombs, attacked and scored a direct hit on an eight-wheeled German armoured car. This was the start of a close association between these two formations, eventually leading to 7 SAAF becoming the second (and unpublicised) 'tank busting' squadron in North Africa.

Two weeks later, the Advanced Air HQ, Egypt, ordered No. 6 Sqn to find out if tanks could also be hunted during the present full moon period, as well as at dawn and dusk. Although some probing flights were made, this 'moonlight' idea was soon forgotten: low-level attacks at night did not appeal to anyone.

Also at this time, the first attempts were made to work

PzKw III at speed with a cloud of dust. (Bundesarchiv)

Desert camouflaged Henschel Hs129B-1 of 8(Pz)/Sch.G2 being towed on a road of the airfield near Tripoli in December 1942. (Bundesarchiv)

out a method of vectoring 'tank busters' onto targets on the ground. A series of exercises lasting five days were started in the Wadi Natrun area beginning 11 October, but the results achieved left much to be desired.

The long expected British offensive began on the night of 23 October 1942 with an artillery barrage from 1,000 guns that lasted for five hours and marked the start of ten days of bitter fighting. Apart from everything else, General Montgomery had also picked the right moment, aware that his opponent Rommel was on sick leave in Germany.

The British numerical and material superiority was impressive: over 1,000 tanks against 200 German and 300 Italian tanks, with odds of three to one in the air.

The two 'tank busting' squadrons were in action the following day. An anti-tank sweep over the southern sector of the El Alamein line brought an interesting score: six captured U.S. Honey (Stuart) light tanks were hit by 6 Sqn and another two Honeys by 7 SAAF Sqn. The same afternoon the score was extended by another eight captured Honeys and two captured Crusader tanks used by the DAK. The maximum armour thickness on both the 19.7-ton Crusader Mk III and the 13.5-ton U.S. Light Tank M3 Stuart (Honey) was 2 in (51 mm). Not a single German-made vehicle was among those hit.

This successful attack was confirmed by some DAK tank soldiers captured later who had witnessed it at close quarters. According to their statements, only six of the 12 Honeys involved were knocked out; the other six managed to return despite several hits in each vehicle. The greatest astonishment

Crusader IICS in the desert in November 1942. (Imperial War Museum)

was to find that shells from aircraft cannon had penetrated hull and turret armour, in some cases passing right through the tank. There being no Axis fighters present, the aircraft had made several attacks; the first had surprised the tank crews, who then baled out and remained in cover till the attacks were over.

The appearance of British 'tank busters' greatly demoralized German troops, and in the future there was often near panic among Axis tank troops whenever low-flying Hurricanes were spotted turning into attack.

According to another POW, about this time Field Marshal Kesselring visited 5 PzRgt to inspect a tank shortly after it had been attacked by British aircraft. All the shells had penetrated the armour, and one of them—believed to be 40 mm calibre—was later sent to Rommel and Kesselring with a report. Although the event cannot be confirmed, there is no doubt that these British 'tank busting' attacks were reported on in detail and influenced similar German developments at that time.

By the night of 2 November 1942, when the British 8th Army began its final attack, the DAK had only 35 medium tanks in fighting condition, with more than 40 in repair. During the following two days the RAF flew some 800 bomber and 500 fighter-bomber sorties per day, while the *Luftwaffe* could only manage about 180. Bravery was no substitute for lack of fuel, ammunition, water and other provisions, and the outcome on the ground was a foregone conclusion. The final Axis retreat began.

Between 24 October and 2 November the two British 'tank busting' squadrons flew 22 sorties on four separate days and claimed five tanks (including two captured Crusaders) and 20 other vehicles, for the loss of two aircraft.

Once the Axis retreat had begun, all the roads leading west were jammed with vehicles of all kinds, but the 'tank busters' were refused permission to join in the hunt. Instead, they were ordered to fly anti-tank sweeps over the southern sector of the El Alamein positions. These 13 sorties increased their claims by one PzKw IV Special, the first of this type attacked by the 'tank busters', plus another five tanks and 34 assorted vehicles.

Five days later, Operation Torch landed American and British troops in Algeria and Tunisia, but for some reason the British 'tank busters' were not called to fly any more sweeps for the next four months. In fact, this change in the official attitude towards these two highly specialised squadrons was evident just

Hurricane IID makes an attack on the German tank on 6 June 1943, during the closing stage of the Tunisian campaign. (Imperial War Museum)

six days after their successful attack south of El Alamein: on 9 November 12 Hurricane IIDs were ordered to be swapped for 12 Hurricane IIC fighters. The following day the 7 SAAF Sqn was ordered back to Shandur for more training, and the 6 Sqn requested to keep six Hurricane IIDs in readiness, but nothing happened. While the fighting grew in intensity in Tunisia, the 'flying tank busters' seemed all but forgotten. Early in December two Flights of the 6 Sqn were ordered back to Egypt to fly shipping protection patrols—quite a comedown for pilots who only a few months earlier had been heroes in the eyes of the Allies.

Without repeating the well-known details of operations leading to the capitulation of the last Axis forces on 13 May 1943, the Tunisian campaign is notable for bringing together several factors of the 'flying tank buster' story: the German Henschel Hs129B armoured ground attack aircraft, which made an inauspicious appearance there; the unexpectedly reactivated 6 Sqn with their Hurricane IID 'tank busters'; the first PzKw IV Tiger tanks met by Western Allies; and, as a direct result, the first Allied use of air-launched rocket projectiles against tanks.

The Hs129B operations in North Africa did not leave a lasting impression: only two *Staffeln* were deployed there, and only one of them did justice to its name.

Apart from the fact that many pilots were still new to the aircraft, the Hs129B was also plagued its French radial engines, which were sensitive to dust ingestion and were difficult to service. The units that flew them were the 4(Pz)/Sch. G 2, which began its brief operational career in Tunisia on 10 November 1942, and the 8(Pz)/Sch.G 2, which had a core of pilots with combat experience on the Eastern Front and was more successful. The latter became operational at El Aouina near Tunis in February 1943 and flew a series of very effective close support and, reportedly, anti-tank sorties, but unfortunately no details are known.

The first six Tiger tanks of 1/sPzAbt 501 (Heavy Tank Detachment) were shipped to Tunisia on 22 November 1942. Ten days later, three of these Tigers participated in a successful attack against the 13 U.S. Armoured Regiment at Tebourba, where the exceptional hitting power of the Tigers' 88 mm guns caused some consternation to the Americans. It also stopped

the immediate Allied threat to Tunis.

Eventually two nearly complete Tiger detachments were deployed in Tunisia, although their 'ready for action' strength never exceeded eight to ten tanks. Nevertheless, this small number possessed exceptional firepower and protection, making the Tigers truly formidable opponents. No Allied tank could withstand the terrific punch of their far-reaching 88 mm gun, and the name 'Tiger' soon had a negative psychological effect on the Allies.

Of course, the Tiger tank was not invulnerable, but it always put up a hard fight. The first Tiger met by the British forces in Tunisia needed six hits from 57 mm anti-tank guns to put it out of action. Another hard-hitting German tank in Tunisia, the latest PzKw IV Ausf. F2 armed with the long-barrelled 75 mm tank gun, was often mistaken for a Tiger.

As the latest British 17-pounder (3 in/76.2 mm) anti-tank guns shipped to North Africa had to be provisionally fitted on 25-pounder field gun carriages (and were not available in sufficient numbers anyway), while the best American anti-tank gun was the 57 mm Ml, a variation of the standard British gun, additional means were needed for the Allies to combat the new German tanks.

This 'Tiger scare' caused the reactivisation of the 'tank busting' 6 Sqn, still flying shipping protection patrols off the Egyptian coast. On 20 February 1943, after some contradictory instructions, 6 Sqn was re-equipped with Hurricane IID 'tank busters' and move to Castel Benito in Libya. Seven days later, the squadron's 18 pilots began intensive firing practices on derelict German tanks scattered around Bir Hacheim.

On 8 March 12 Hurricane IIDs of 6 Sqn were transferred to Hazbub Satellite landing ground, where they saw action the following day. Their first target was a German armoured column that had attempted to dislodge some Free French forces at Ksar Rhilare, behind the Mareth Line. In repeated low-level attacks the Hurricane IIDs with their 40 mm cannon practically annihilated the German force, and their day's score was most impressive: six PzKw III tanks, 13 armoured vehicles and 20 other motor vehicles hit and partly set on fire, at an Allied loss of just two crash-landed and one combat damaged Hurricane IID. A week later, the 'tank busting' activities of 6 Sqn were mentioned in a BBC broadcast, and the world at large was again aware of their existence.

During the remaining two months of fighting in Tunisia the 6 Sqn participated in another 14 missions, flying 115 sorties and claiming hits on 26 PzKw IV (none destroyed) and 37 PzKw III tanks (17 destroyed), as well as 35 other vehicles and guns. In the process 25 Hurricane IIDs were shot down, and three pilots were lost.

For inexplicable reasons most of these attacks were flown without any fighter cover, despite the fact that there must have been fighters to spare in Tunisia at that time.

On 9 April 1943, a few weeks before their last operation, seven 6 Sqn pilots were decorated with the coveted DFC (Distinguished Flying Cross)—including Flying Officer D. W. Jones, the American volunteer still with the unit and the first American 'tank buster' of World War II.

Official 6 Sqn records do not specifically mention any attacks on Tiger tanks. Apart from some lucky hits, their 40 mm cannon shells could not have been effective against these well-armoured targets. However, by autumn 1942 another British weapon had reached the operational stage—the air-launched rocket projectile. Developed from the 3 in (76.2 mm) anti-aircraft barrage rocket, the anti-tank version was fitted with a 25 lb (11.3 kg) solid steel warhead which, under test conditions, could punch through a 100 mm armour plate. Although not very accurate due to its drop and dispersion, the launching aircraft could carry four of the early RPs under each wing, and the chances of hitting a tank seemed better than even.

Late in November 1942 six tropicalised Hurricane II fighters fitted with Mk I rocket launching rails were urgently and secretly despatched to North Africa. This new rocket sextet was accompanied by several trial pilots who trained the first service pilots in the idiosyncrasies of their new weapon. The first rocket attack on German armour followed a short while later and shocked all concerned: the tanks, which turned out to be the new Tigers, did not seem to be affected even by several direct hits. The 25 lb AP (Armour Piercing) rocket with a solid steel warhead was obviously not powerful enough; something else was needed.

An urgent re-examination of the anti-tank rocket projectile situation ensued. First, the problem of 'scatter' was addressed. The difficulties in aiming rocket projectiles due to their drift were known from trials, but the problem became even more pronounced under combat conditions, especially when the pilot had to take evasive action. For one thing, the RPs tended to follow the line of flight, which was not the same as the line of sight. Even if this drift factor could be overcome (as it was, with special pilot training), the 25 lb AP rocket had to hit the tank in certain places to disable it. Apart from making a lucky hit from a salvo, the pilot would have to go in closer to score, thus defeating the purpose of the rocket-armed aircraft.

The second problem involved a lack of penetration power. One obvious solution was the use of hollow-charge rocket warheads, but the development of British warheads of this type had run into problems from the beginning and all further work had been stopped late in 1941.

At this stage the ordinary 60 lb (27 kg) HE (high explosive) rocket warhead was tried against tanks and found most effective: only one hit was needed to destroy any tank, while a near miss was practically guaranteed to rip the tank's tracks and immobilise it. The 60 lb HE warhead also proved

Ground crew holding a 60 lb (27 kg) HE rocket in front of No. 6 Squadron's Hurricane Mk IV. (Imperial War Museum)

most destructive against other ground targets, including fortifications. The operational trials led to a complete reversal of the originally intended use of the rocket warheads. From then on, the 25 lb AP (and SAP) were employed exclusively against shipping targets, while the 60 lb HE rocket projectile became the favourite anti-tank weapon.

During the Tunisian campaign, which ended on 13 May 1943, many lessons were learned.

According to official 6 Sqn records, its pilots flew 319 anti-tank sorties during three operational periods: 8 June 1942–29 September 1942; 2 October 1942–6 April 1943 (with 7 SAAF Sqn); and 7 April–7 May 1943. Their total hits included 144 tanks (47 destroyed); 34 armoured cars (five destroyed); 17 half-tracks (three destroyed); and 126 other vehicles and guns hit and/or destroyed, including 103 trucks.

(Most often 40 mm cannon hits from 'tank busters' only disabled an armoured fighting vehicle. The German tank recovery service in North Africa was very efficient and usually salvaged the damaged vehicles)

The 6 Sqn losses included 47 Hurricane IIDs (40 in action, seven in flying accidents) and seven pilots (five killed in action, two in accidents). Of the 40 Hurricane IIDs lost in action, only one was shot down by a fighter (Bf109); all the others fell victim to ground fire—clear proof of how vulnerable the unarmoured Hurricane was in low-level flight. Unfortunately, the urgent need for 'tank busters' in North Africa did not leave any time to devise suitable armour protection. In fact, it was not until late in 1942 that an attempt was made to remedy this situation, but no armour-protected Hurricane IIDs ever reached North Africa.

Tank busters on the Eastern Front

'Unternehmen Barbarossa', the German invasion of the Soviet Union, began at 0330 hrs on Sunday, 22 June 1941. This most expansive, bloodiest and, as it turned out, final German campaign of World War II has been described and analysed in detail in many publications. This narrative will only cover the events which led to the creation of the special 'flying tank busters' and their subsequent operations and development.

For that reason it is of interest first to compare the strength and quality of the opposing armour and anti-tank defences on that fateful day.

Germany: 3,332 tanks of various types in 17 Panzer divisions organised into four Panzer Groups, including 13 motorised infantry and one cavalry divisions. Additionally, the German Army fielded 250 assault guns on PzKw III chassis for infantry support.

The combat quality of this German armour was another matter. Of the 3,332 tanks deployed in the East, only 2,176 were really fit for the task: 439 PzKw IVs, 965 PzKw IIIs and 772 PzKw 38(t)s (the Czech-built LT 38), which equipped five German Panzer divisions. The remaining 1,156 tanks included the thinly-armoured PzKw I (410) and PzKw II (746), no match even for the second-line Soviet tanks. As this campaign was confidently expected to be over by Christmas 1941, the tanks' poor combat quality did not seem to matter to the Germans.

The standard German anti-tank gun in June 1941 was still the 37 mm Pak 35/36. Based on experiences in Spain, work on a more powerful anti-tank gun began in 1937, but it was not until April 1941 that the first examples of the 50 mm Pak 38 entered service. It was able to penetrate 78 mm of armour at 500 m (550 yds) and 61 mm at 1,000 m (1,100 yds) at 0° impact, but too few Pak 38s were in service in June 1941 to meet the demand. Also, its best performance occurred when it was fitted with a tungsten-cored shell, but that metal was in increasingly short supply in Germany.

Soviet Union: At least 24,000 tanks of all types (German Intelligence estimate: 10,000), with about 16,000 in the Western regions. However, this enormous inventory of armour—more than the rest of the world put together—varied in quality, ranging from dated light tanks to the very latest models. Proper organisational and command structures needed to be strengthened and the 29 newly formed mechanised corps were still in a state of flux.

On 22 June 1941 the core of this force consisted of 1,503 tanks superior to anything the Germans had at the time, 1,110 new T-34s and 393 of the heavier KV-1s, the existence of which was completely unknown to German Intelligence. Next in combat quality came the BT-5/-7 series of fast tanks, at least 4,000 of which were available. The standard Soviet infantry support tank was still the T-26, and several thousand of them were in service. In addition, the Soviets possessed several hundred assorted heavy and medium tanks, including several regiments equipped with the 52-ton KV-2 heavy support tank.

The most important Soviet tank was the T-34, which greatly influenced future operations on the Eastern Front and tank design in general. Like the other Soviet war-winning weapon, the Ilyushin Il-2 *Shturmovik*, the T-34 was built in large numbers. Despite the forced evacuation of the principal tank manufacturing facilities, the production drive was such that

Two rows of Ilyushin Il-2s fill the assembly lines in 1942. (Novosti Press)

during the period July to December 1941, Soviet industry delivered 1,853 T-34s, 728 KV-1s and 1,548 T-60 light tanks. By then, the main T-34 factory was at Chelyabinsk east of the Ural mountains. The factory would become an enormous manufacturing facility known as Tankograd. Production plans drawn up in November 1941 envisioned an average annual output of 22,000 tanks and 25,000 combat aircraft of all types.

Initially, the potentially superior T-34 and KV-1 tanks were badly misused in scattered attacks on German forces, although the KV-1 was never as much of a threat as the sleek, agile T-34. It took nine months of increasingly bitter defensive fighting before the Soviet commanders had a chance to assimilate their experiences in tank warfare. Soon, stronger groups of T-34s began to form the spearhead of nearly all Soviet attacks and, together with the less numerous but better protected KV-1 tanks, became the main cause behind the urgent German need for effective anti-tank measures on the Eastern Front, culminating in the 'flying tank busters' after the Stalingrad debacle.

Apart from having a slightly larger calibre, Soviet anti-tank guns in June 1941 were similar to those of their German opponents. The standard Soviet anti-tank gun, the 45 mm L/45 M1932, was a scaled-up version of the 37 mm Rheinmetall anti-tank gun built under licence and able to penetrate just 50 mm of armour at 500 m (550 yrds) at 0° impact. Design of a more potent anti-tank gun began after the Spanish Civil War and advanced rapidly. This 57 mm L/73 weapon was a great improvement and could penetrate 140 mm of armour at 500 m at 0° impact (sufficient to knock out any known tank), but it was not scheduled to enter Red Army service until June 1941, just before the German attack.

On *Barbarossa* day, the attacking German forces were supported by 2,875 aircraft, but only 1,945 were suitable for combat. There were no modern ground support aircraft designed for the purpose, and 'tank hunting' aircraft were unheard of. The additional 890 Rumanian, Hungarian, Croatian and later Finnish and Italian aircraft were of varying quality and only of local significance.

Opposing them were an estimated 8,000 Soviet aircraft. More than half were outdated, and only 1,540 new types were in service in the Western regions on that day. Among this number were the first 70 Il-2 *Shturmovik*s (out of 249 delivered to the Soviet Air Force), aircraft that had no counterpart in the *Luftwaffe* or any other air force. With the T-34 tank and the BM-13 *'Katyusha'* multiple rocket launcher, the Il-2 added

Single-seated Il-2s over Russia. (Imperial War Museum)

a new dimension to warfare.

The confusion created by the German attack was so great that practically anything that came to hand was thrown into battle to try to stem the advancing Panzer columns. New weapons were not exempted. Instead of holding them back until their crews had a chance to familiarise themselves with their new equipment and a numerous force had been built up, the Soviets made use of the Il-2 *Shturmovik* and the T-34 and KV-1 tanks during the first week of fighting.

The effect of these Soviet weapons on the morale of ordinary German soldiers was serious. The BM-13 multiple rocket launcher caused them similar concern. Never slow to coin humorous expressions to hide bitter experience, the German frontline soldier soon developed one for his now useless 37 mm anti-tank gun: 'The Army Doorknocker'. It was being replaced by the new 50 mm Pak 38, but even this new gun had a hard time knocking out the well-armoured, low-slung and fast-moving Soviet tanks.

While the high-level German leadership was loath to admit that the Russians could have produced something superior, the military experts took a different view. Tests of captured T-34 tanks deeply impressed German tank officers and designers alike: the sloping armour and the shape of the hull and turret were practically ideal; the aluminum alloy diesel engine a revelation; the 76 mm high-velocity gun as good as anything on their side and the sturdy wide tracks on the modified Christie-type suspension were ideal for the Russian terrain. Additionally, the T-34 had obvious development potential.

The Germans urgently needed a new medium tank that could beat the T-34 in combat. Their solution was the PzKw V Panther; its design was approved by Hitler on 12 May 1942 from two projects submitted. The influence of the Soviet

T-34/76B (Model 1941) tanks in the Red Square on 7 November 1941. (Novosti Press)

KV-1 heavy tanks start for the battlefield in 1942. (Novosti Press)

progenitor is unmistakable, although the new Panther was no mere adaptation of the T-34. Once its teething troubles were mastered, the Panther became the best all-round medium tank of World War II.

But all that was still in the future. In summer 1941, tanks and especially 'tank fright' also occupied the minds of Soviet commanders. Only tanks could force a decision on the battlefield, as constantly demonstrated by the German Panzer formations, which would crash through the Soviet lines seemingly at will and then strike deep into the hinterland. Soviet anti-tank guns and artillery were clearly inadequate, and anti-tank mines and tank ditches were only a temporary solution. Something more mobile was needed.

While the first part of these conclusions were identical to those later reached by the German command, Soviet anti-tank measures did not have to rely so much on improvisation: the Il-2 *Shturmovik* was already on hand.

The first Soviet Air Force unit to be equipped with the new single-seat Il-2 was 4 ShAP (*Shturmovoi Aviapolk*, Assault Aviation Rgt) late in May 1941. By then, the urgency was such that pilots familiarised themselves with their new mounts at the factory before being deployed to Bogodukhov, near Kharkov. By mid-June 1941, 4 ShAP had only 15 aircraft for combat, out of a total strength of 65 Il-2s.

The 4 ShAP was soon joined by the 215 ShAP, the first to use the Il-2 in combat. Although lacking details, the following report of this action is of considerable interest as a representative description of early *Shturmovik* attacks:

'In mid-June, just after the completion of our training on the Il's, we were deployed westwards. At that time the area west of Yartsevo-Velikiye Luki was the scene of much confused and bitter fighting, and we were ordered on our first operational sortie just after landing at our new base. The target was a large column of German armour established by our aerial recce west of Velikiye Luki; they had obviously broken through the main combat lines and were now moving our way.

The seven available Il-2s (the rest of 215 ShAP was still being fitted out) under Capt Gvozdev, Deputy CO of the Rgt, were led to the target by a Pe-2 bomber. The German armoured column was found exactly where reported.

On commander's orders, we followed him down towards the German tanks and other vehicles. The procedure was to drop the bombs first, then turn and come back from another direction, releasing the RS-82 rockets and opening fire with our wing cannon and machine guns while in a shallow attack dive.

Our attack came as a complete surprise to the German troops on the ground and was quite successful. Capt Gvozdev's bombs scored a direct hit on one of the German tanks and a covered truck beside it, blowing it across the road and blocking it. Light German Flak protecting the column fired furiously but too late and too wide. As planned, we left the scene at low level and came back from the other side, letting loose with our RS-82s and wing guns. Tanks and other vehicles on the blocked road were hit time and again and

German highly effective anti-aircraft weapons, the 2 cm *Flakvierling* 38. (Bundesarchiv)

Il-2 passes through over German troops in the autumn of 1941. (Bundesarchiv)

caught fire and truckloads of ammunition were exploding all over the place. That stopped the advancing German column! We re-assembled outside the range of the German Flak and turned back to our base. Out first assault had been successfully carried out.'

From the above it is evident that in summer 1941 the Il-2s were so urgently needed that pilot training was limited to learning to fly the aircraft and a few evasive manoeuvres. There was no time to teach more than basic navigation (note the Pe-2 'leader' across the lines). Likewise, there had been no time to work out special attack formations or assault tactics; it was simply a matter of 'follow the leader.' For some time only the 'commanding' Il-2s had radio sets—and those were of less than reliable quality. Nobody had yet either run the gauntlet of light German Flak or tried to turn with the fighters. Neither was there a fighter escort as the heavily armoured *Shturmovik*s were considered capable of looking after themselves.

Over the next few weeks sudden *Shturmovik* attacks were repeated all along the Central Front where the first Il-2 units were concentrated.

But once the surprise element of these sudden assaults had passed, the German armoured formations took care to keep in close radio contact with neighbouring units to pass warnings of any 'heavy single-engined aircraft' sighted and to have motorised light Flak positioned forward with the tanks. Experience showed the importance of flank observations as the Soviet assault aircraft never flew across the front line directly towards their target. A few months later the German mechanised troops began to receive their first 20 mm *Flakvierling* 38 four-barrelled light anti-aircraft guns. These effective weapons were dreaded by low-level attack pilots, and Il-2 losses began to mount. Although the main targets of the Il-2s were the German armour, there were no specific Soviet 'tank hunting' units until 1943.

As a rule, German mechanised/motorised columns had their own light anti-aircraft guns, but infantry on foot and columns of horse-drawn vehicles were at the mercy of the *Shturmovik*s, nicknamed 'The Black Death.'

The Il-2 was by no means invulnerable or invincible. A single-seater that flew at bomber speed, it was easy to intercept and, lacking any rear defence, to shoot down. If caught unprotected, Il-2 pilots were trained to react by forming a closed defensive circle, slowly 'moving' it towards their own territory. To form such a circle at least six aircraft were needed, flying 300 to 400 m (330 to 440 yds) apart at an altitude of not less than 300 m and banking at 15–20° angle. There were occasions when individual Il-2s turned to face their pursuers, but such events were rare. Their only chance was to fly as low as possible, using the terrain to their advantage if the ground was not flat, as was often the case. As shown later, even fighter escort could

Hawker Hurricane Mk IID attacking PzKpfw IV Ausf. Ds on the North African Front.

Claims of No. 6 Squadron during three operational periods (319 operational sorties in all. See page 13)
 1 PzKw IV Ausf. F2 ('Panzer IV Special')—hit
21 PzKw IVs: 15 hit, 6 destroyed
 1 PzKW III Ausf. J ('Panzer III Special')—hit
65 PzKw IIIs: 42 hit, 23 destroyed
 5 PzKw IIs—destroyed
14 Italian M13s: 6 destroyed
 6 captured Crusader tanks—hit
19 captured Stuart (Honey) tanks: 13 hit, 6 destroyed
12 unidentified tanks—hit
34 armored cars: 29 hit, 5 destroyed
17 half-tracks: 14 hit, 3 destroyed
and 126 other vehicles and guns hit and/or destroyed

Henschel Hs129B-2/R2

belongs to 8 *Panzerjägerstaffel* of *Schlachtgeschwader* 2 on the
Eastern Front in the summer of 1943. 8(Pz)/Sch.G 2 was redesignated
13(Pz)/SG 9 on October 18, 1943.
Fixed armament
1 × 30 mm MK 103 cannon with 100 rounds
2 × 20 mm MG 151/20 cannon with 125 rounds per gun
2 × 13 mm MG 131 machine guns with 300 rounds per gun
Bombs
2 × AB 70D1 containers loaded with 50 × 1 kg (2.2 lb) SD 1 anti-personnel bombs each

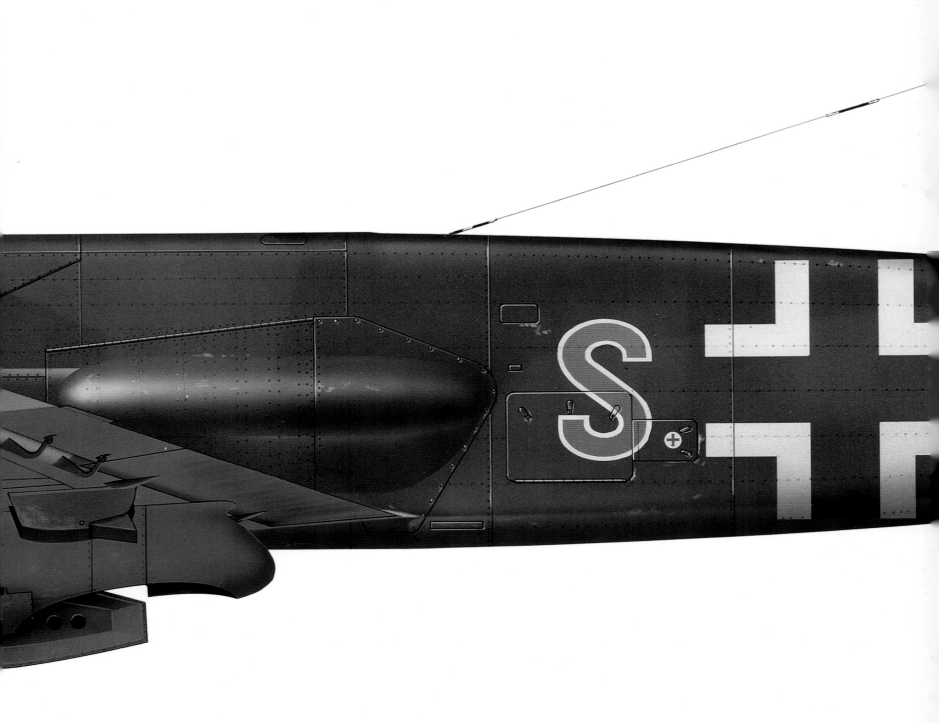

Aircraft corresponding to the technical data here will be found on the reverse side of this stretch-out

Junkers Ju87G-1s, belong to *Panzerjägerstaffel* (led by *Hauptmann* Hans-Ulrich Rudel) of *Sturzkampfgeschwader* 2 *"Immelmann"*, attack Russian Tank T-34 Model 1943s of the 41st Guards Tank Brigade, 7th Mechanized Corps, in Kursk area on the Eastern Front in July 1943, during *Unternehmen 'Zitadelle'* (Operational Citadel).

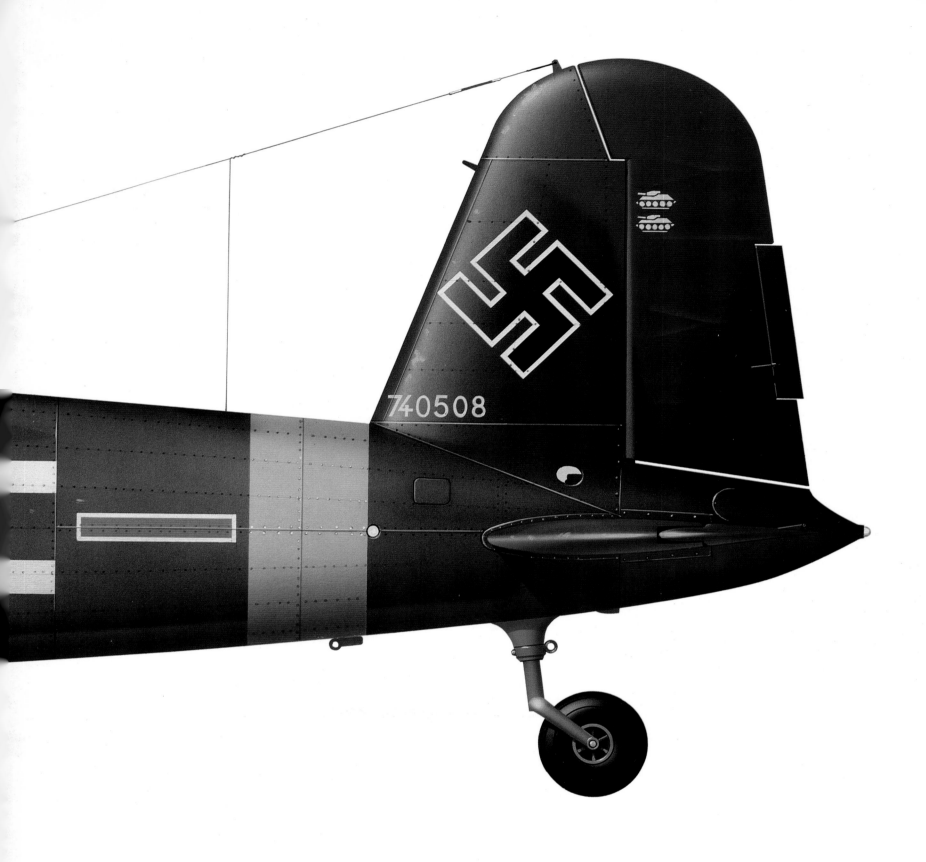

Reinmetall-Borsig 37 mm BK 3.7 anti-tank cannon
under the wing of Ju87G-1
Length of weapon: 3.626 m (11 ft 10³/₄ in) with muzzle brake
Length of barrel: 2.112 m (6 ft 11¹/₈ in)
Weight of weapon: 272 kg (600 lb)
                  343 kg (756 lb) complete in fixed installation
Weight of barrel: 66.8 kg (147.3 lb)
Muzzle velocity: 795–860 m (2,608–2,822 ft)/sec according to ammunition
Rate of fire: 140 rpm
System of operation: Recoil
Ammunition capacity: 2 × 6 rounds (per cannon for Ju87G)
Armor penetration: 58 mm at 60° at 100 m (330 ft)
                   120 mm at 60° at 100 m (330 ft) with special hard-core
                   ammunition
Effective firing range: 2,000 m (6,600 ft)
Remarks: Modified Flak 18 anti-aircraft gun with shortened barrel, in turn
developed from Solothurn S10-100 gun.

Medium Tank T-34 Model 1943
Engine: 1 × V-2-34 12-cylinder diesel, 500 hp
Combat weight: 30,900 kg (68,120 lb)
Length, overall: 6.75 m (22 ft 1³/₄ in)
Length, excluding gun: 6.1 m (20 ft)
Height: 2.60 m (8 ft 6³/₈ in)
Armor: 20–70 mm
Max speed by road: 55 km/h (34.2 mph)
Max speed across country: 40 km/h (24.9 mph)
Range by road: 290 km (180 mls)
Range across country: 200 km (125 mls)
Armament: 1 × 76.2 mm F-34 Model 1942 L/42 gun with 100 rounds
          2 × 7.62 mm DT machine guns with 3,600 rounds in all
          Without anti-aircraft machine gun

Crew: 4

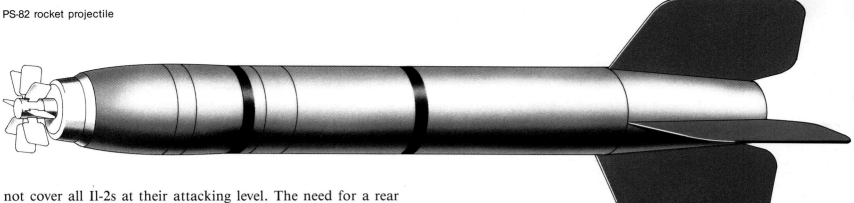

not cover all Il-2s at their attacking level. The need for a rear gunner was evident, but it took another 15 months before something was done to remedy this fatal weakness.

Another inherent deficiency of the early Il-2 was its primitive VV-1 sight with a bead mounted on top of the engine cowling and sighting lines engraved in the 55 mm armour glass windscreen. This sight was used to aim both the guns and the rocket projectiles. As the RS-82s could not be relied upon to fly straight and level for more than 200 m (220 yds), the *Shturmovik* pilot had to get very near his target to hit even a stationary tank, thus minimising his own chances of survival.

The evolution of assault tactics, especially against armoured fighting vehicles, the primary target, was learned from hard experience. Despite the long history of Soviet *Shturmovik* aviation, only the basic low-level attack guidelines were of any practical use. The Il-2 had introduced a new element on the battlefield, and the new tactics had to relate to armoured columns protected by mobile anti-aircraft guns and to defended point targets behind enemy lines.

Once the Il-2 had proved its effectiveness against German armoured fighting vehicles and other ground targets, every effort was made to boost its production. No Soviet contingency plan had foreseen an enemy penetrating Soviet territory so deeply, and suddenly hundreds of war plants had to be moved out of reach of the German bombers. By a stroke of good fortune, most available *Luftwaffe* bombers were committed to army support tasks, and so the slow-moving evacuation trains were hardly interferred with.

The evacuation naturally had an adverse effect on the output of aircraft and tanks in particular. Production was limited to a small number of selected aircraft types with the Il-2 *Shturmovik* topping this list. During the second half of 1941 1,293 Il-2s were completed and delivered. In late November/December 1941, a German advance on Moscow was held just outside the suburbs of the Soviet capital. Output of essential war materials was at its lowest ebb, and hasty assembly and bad workmanship caused many Il-2s to be delivered to operational units in unserviceable condition. Factory management was taken to task in no uncertain manner. On 23 December 1941 Shenkman, director of the principal Il-2 plant (GAZ No. 18), received a sharply worded telegram from Stalin, stating in part, 'The Il-2 is as vital to our Red Army as air and bread…If GAZ No. 18 thinks it can fob us off with one Il-2 per day it is cruelly mistaken and will suffer the consequences…I demand the production of more Il-2s. This is my last warning. Stalin.' Drastic measures were immediately taken to increase output, and Il-2 production soon began to rise. A total of 2,620 were completed during the first six months of 1942, and output was more than doubled during the second half of that year with 5,596 Il-2s completed.

Although the bravery of *Shturmovik* pilots won open German respect, nothing could disguise the fact that the single-seat Il-2 was a vulnerable aircraft despite its strong armour protection. The Il-2 attrition rate for 1941 was very high and was tacitly admitted by the Soviet command at that time when they awarded the title 'Hero of the Soviet Union' to Il-2 pilots who had flown just ten operational sorties.

There were also problems relating to armament. The RS-82 or RS-132 rocket projectiles in drag-inducing underwing clusters, inaccurate and unreliable as they were, were still far more effective than trying to hit tanks with bombs or 20 mm cannon fire. Late in 1941 a special ground attack version was introduced, the RBS-132.

On urgent recommendation, the Il-2 was modified in February 1942 to combine both the more powerful AM-38F engine and a rudimentary cockpit for a rear gunner armed with a flexible 12.7 mm Beresin UBT machine gun. This emergency conversion was completed in just three weeks and could be applied to single-seat Il-2s on the production line and to those already in service. Soon afterwards, work began on a new *Shturmovik*. This line led to two parallel developments, the Il-8 and the Il-10, the latter of which eventually replaced the Il-2.

Although only marginally stable, the new field-conversion Il-2 two-seaters were the best that could be fashioned at that time. They were first used operationally in August 1942 over the Stalingrad area. The factory-produced Il-2M two-seaters made their combat debut over the Central Front on 30 October 1942. During their early sorties these two-seat Il-2s had some success against the German fighter pilots who mistakenly assumed them to be ordinary single-seaters with no rear defence, but that did not last long. Combat reports and details of shotdown Il-2s were speedily circulated, and their losses began to mount again.

The pattern of subsequent aerial assaults began to change early in 1942 when the Il-2 production started to catch up with losses. There were never enough *Luftwaffe* fighters to intercept all attacking *Shturmovik*s. As a result, damage to German tanks caught near the main combat line was greater: one rocket projectile of a salvo of eight was almost bound to hit, no matter how inaccurate the rockets were individually.

The definitive Il-2 two-seat version was designated the Il-2 *tip* 3 (usually described as Il-2m3), which was an attempt to cure some of its predecessors negative characteristics such as poor stability and sluggish response to controls. Sergei Ilyushin, who was given a free hand provided his modifications did not disrupt the production, ruled out a complete redesign. His solution was the best remedy under the circumstances: a 15° sweep-back of the outer wing panels, which transferred lift aft and compensated for the center of gravity movement. Official trials with the Il-2 *tip* 3 were completed on 12 December 1942, by which time the new version was already in production. The Il-2 *tip* 3 was first flown in combat late in January 1943 in the Stalingrad area and was to become the most widely built variant of the basic design.

The organisation and establishment of 'assault aviation' units changed according to circumstances. The original summer 1941 strength of an assault aviation regiment included three squadrons with reserves and totalled 65 aircraft. No Il-2 regiment ever reached that strength. A general reorganisation of Soviet Air Force formations began in August 1941, but the *Shturmovik* units had to be considered separately. In late October 1941 a theoretical assault aviation regiment consisted of 33 aircraft (including ten fighters and two 'leaders'). Only months later, all regiments equipped with 'new aircraft types' were standardised to include only 20 aircraft (in the case of *Shturmovik*s, including two 'leaders'), although the heavy losses of late 1941/early 1942 meant that in practice most Il-2 regiments could field only 12–15 aircraft.

In 1942, with the availability of more Il-2s, the assault aviation regiments were gradually expanded to three squadrons, about 30 aircraft. No attempt was made to revert to the 1941 establishment. In fact, the new Soviet air regiment was modelled on the *Luftwaffe Gruppe* and could operate just as independently having only administrative ties to its division.

The *Luftwaffe Rotte/Schwarm* (pair/'finger four') combat formation, evolved in Spain by the leading German fighter ace Werner Mölders, was introduced in Soviet fighter aviation in the summer of 1942 and from late that summer was also increasingly used by Il-2 formations. Subsequent organisational changes led to the establishment of assault aviation divisions (ShAD) and, in mid-1943, assault aviation corps (ShAK).

Apart from the initial shock of encountering the T-34 and KV-1 tanks during the early clashes in 1941, the German armed forces began to experience their first 'tank fears' early in 1942 after the collapse of their attack on Moscow. This was the first time they had been checked and forced to retreat on a large scale. The Soviet counterattack north and south of Moscow began on 6 December 1941 and soon broke through the weakened German lines in several places. Swelled by an increasing number of fresh formations transferred from the Far East, it gained momentum and developed into a counteroffensive that was to spread all along the Eastern Front and last until March 1942. It was the first time German troops had to deal with Soviet tanks that had penetrated far behind their lines, often in most unfavourable weather conditions, causing havoc. Once through the defended zone, any tank, no matter how old, was a mobile gun that could pose a serious threat.

Before mobile German anti-tank guns and 'flying tank busters' were available, this situation often led to desperate anti-tank measures by the German frontline troops.

At this time Soviet tanks began to carry small sections of assault infantry armed with sub-machine guns. Known as *tankovoi desant* (tank-borne landing troops), their life expectancy was short, but they provided immediate protection for the tanks and joined in ground combat. Intended as a substitute for armoured personnel carriers, these 'tank riders' became a permanent feature of Soviet tank attacks.

These developments caught the German command unprepared. Having wrongly estimated available Soviet tank strength, the situation was compounded by another fatal assessment regarding the revival of Soviet tank production.

When the general Soviet counteroffensive began early in 1942, many Flak guns, available because of the lack of aerial targets, were impressed into the anti-tank role. Only the 88 mm guns were really effective, but their number behind the frontline was not great.

The *Luftwaffe*, already fully committed to ground support tasks, was often called in to bomb Soviet tank concentrations. It was clear that this was a wasteful and inefficient way to combat tanks from the air, and other means had to be found.

The use of larger-calibre cannon or possibly Army-type rocket projectiles against Soviet tanks was first proposed by several *Luftwaffe* frontline officers, but similar developments were already in hand, initiated before the Soviet winter offensive. The German counterpart to the Soviet *Shturmovik* was about to appear over the battlefield.

Series production of the Hs129B-1 began in January 1942, at the height of the Soviet winter counteroffensive. This first production version incorporated a number of features in line with current *Luftwaffe* practice, such as 20 mm MG 151/20 cannon with electrically fired cartridges and provision for several *Rüstsätze* (equipment or armament sets) that could be fitted or replaced by maintenance personnel in the field. This facility greatly extended the Hs129B's potential and included a special 'tank hunting' set, the R2, comprising one long-barrelled 30 mm MK 101 automatic cannon with a 30-round magazine in a streamlined underfuselage pannier.

For its time, the MK 101 was a powerful and accurate weapon. It could fire nine different types of ammunition ranging from ordinary high-explosive to tungsten-cored armour-piercing shells. The latter had a 231 g tungsten-carbide core which could penetrate 75 mm of armour plating at 300 m (330 yds) and 103 mm at 50 m (55 yds) range, very good values for a 30 mm cannon. Unfortunately tungsten was in short supply in Germany, and due to hurried training of future Hs129 pilots, wastage of this precious ammunition was unavoidable.

The first unit to be equipped with the Hs129B-1 was the newly-formed 4/Sch.G 1 at Lippstadt which received 16 aircraft in April 1942 and left for the Eastern Front on 10 May 1942. Two days later, very strong Soviet forces, commanded by

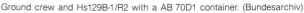

Ground crew and Hs129B-1/R2 with a AB 70D1 container. (Bundesarchiv)

An armorer loading 20 mm ammunition for Hs129B-1/R2's MG 151/20. (Bundesarchiv)

The 30 mm Mk 108 cannon fitted to beneath the fuselage of Hs129B-1/R2. (Bundesarchiv)

Marshal Timoshenko, broke out of their bridgehead west of the Donets River, but on 17 May they were temporarily checked by a flanking German counterattack. On the same day, Timoshenko committed his main striking force, the 21 Tank Corps, to an attack. There was soon a crisis on the battlefield. At this stage the Hs129Bs were called in to help deal with the Soviet armour and test their MK 101 cannon in action, with telling effect. According to subsequent statements by Soviet POWs, the new Hs129Bs 'not only put tanks out of action but also caused panic among the Soviet troops'. The Hs129Bs also achieved good results during the following Soviet retreat when attacks were carried out in waves of up to 20 aircraft. During these operations 4/Sch.G 1 claimed the destruction of 23 Soviet tanks, and the *Geshwader* command requested more cannon-armed Hs129Bs.

However, after the battle there were some doubts about the effectiveness of the MK 101 and its armour-piercing ammunition: no Soviet tanks knocked out by aircraft cannon could be found among the many destroyed on the battlefield. The pilots were naturally disappointed and asked for the MK 101 cannon to be removed and replaced by bomb racks. Weeks went by before any official reaction was made to the request.

The summer of 1942 was marked by two great battles: the second German assault on and capture of Sevastopol with its almost indestructable fortifications (7 June–2 July) and the German summer offensive. The latter started on 28 June and made very rapid progress. Less than a month later it split into a spearhead pointing at Stalingrad and a more southerly drive towards the Caucasus and the Soviet oil wells. There was no real need for 'flying tank busters' during these summer offensives, and this respite was used to try to cure some of the ills of the Hs129B, in particular the sensitivity of its French-radial engines to dust. A reasonably effective filter was developed in a few weeks, but not much could be done about the unreliable performance of these power plants.

In late June 1942 plans were also drawn up to establish more Hs129B-equipped units by forming a *Panzerjägerstaffel* as an integral part of each *Jagdgeschwader* on the Eastern Front, but only JG 51 managed to do so. In this case, there were no complaints about the MK 101 cannon, and this separate 'tank hunting' unit achieved quite a respectable record. Between 11 August and 26 September 1942, starting with eight Hs129B-1s, it flew 16 operations against Soviet tanks in the Rzhev area and in a total of 73 sorties claimed to have hit 29 tanks at the loss of just three aircraft.

By this time reports about the disenchantment of 4/Sch.G 1 pilots with their MK 101 cannon had reached higher levels. The criticisms affected the planned introduction of cannon-armed anti-tank aircraft, and an armaments expert was sent to II/Sch.G 1 and the *Panzerjägerstaffel* of JG 51 late in September 1942 to investigate the complaints and convince the pilots of the effectiveness of cannon attacks if properly carried out. It was a belated attempt to rectify the lack of sufficient training in the use of this new weapon. Although the MK 101 armament set (R2) had been introduced early in 1942, there was no organised training until early September, and the pilots were left to their own devices. Other complaints included a lack of qualified armourers to look after the MK 101 and a lack of spare parts.

Pilots of the *Panzerjägerstaffel* of JG 51, on the other hand, had used the lull in fighting to carry out intensive training, achieving a 60 percent hit record. Successful practice attacks had also been flown against captured Soviet tanks. Exercises were also carried out with Army units in radio contact to ensure that anti-tank and ground-support aircraft would be on the spot when needed.

It was a different story at 4/Sch.G 1 which, together with the rest of II/Sch.G 1, was based at Millerovo in mid-November 1942 with 20 serviceable Hs129B-1s and 10 Bf109Es, all equipped as bombers. Once the misuse of the Hs129B had become known, the Inspector of Ground Support Aviation immediately ordered the removal of all bomb racks and their replacement by MK 101 cannon sets, followed by an intensive training period for the pilots. There was a widespread impression that a tank was only effectively hit if it was set on fire, and in order to achieve this many Hs129B pilots would use up their whole ammunition supply (30 rounds) attacking a single tank, even when hits by the magnesium-tipped shells could be clearly seen. It took some persuasion to convince the pilots that it was not necessary to set the tank on fire: what counted was the penetration of its armour which killed or disabled the crew. This called for steady flying, accurate shooting and closing in for better observation of hits—not always possible under battle conditions. Training was the key, but there was no chance to catch up on lost time.

By late November the twin-pronged Soviet counter-offensive at Stalingrad, timed to coincide with the Western Allied landing in North Africa and the onset of local frost to faciliate cross-country tank movement, was already in full swing, and strong Soviet tank spearheads were rapidly advancing towards the Donets. Although wiser after the first Russian

Junkers Ju87G-1 Cutaway

1 Spinner
2 Pitch-change counterweights
3 Junkers VS11 constant speed propeller
4 Junkers Jumo211J-1 12-cylinder inverted-vee liquid-cooled engine
5 Oil filler panel
6 Auxiliary oil tank (26.8 ltr/7.1 U.S. gal/5.9 Imp gal)
7 Coolant (Glysantin-water) header tank
8 Ejector exhaust stubs
9 Armored coolant radiator (center)
10 Oil cooler

11 Magnesium alloy forged engine mount
12 Engine accessories
13 Firewall bulkhead
14 Main oil tank (45 ltr/11.9 U.S. gal/9.9 Imp gal)
15 Rudder pedals
16 Ventral vision panel
17 Ventral vision panel control
18 Engine control runs
19 Throttle lever
20 Tail trim control handle
21 Control stick
22 Oil filler panel
23 Oil tank (31 ltr/8.2 U.S. gal/6.8 Imp gal)
24 Fresh air intake flap
25 Reinforced armored windscreen
26 Revi C/12C or C/12D reflector sight
27 De-icing air intake flap
28 Handholds
29 Padded crash bar
30 Switchbox

28

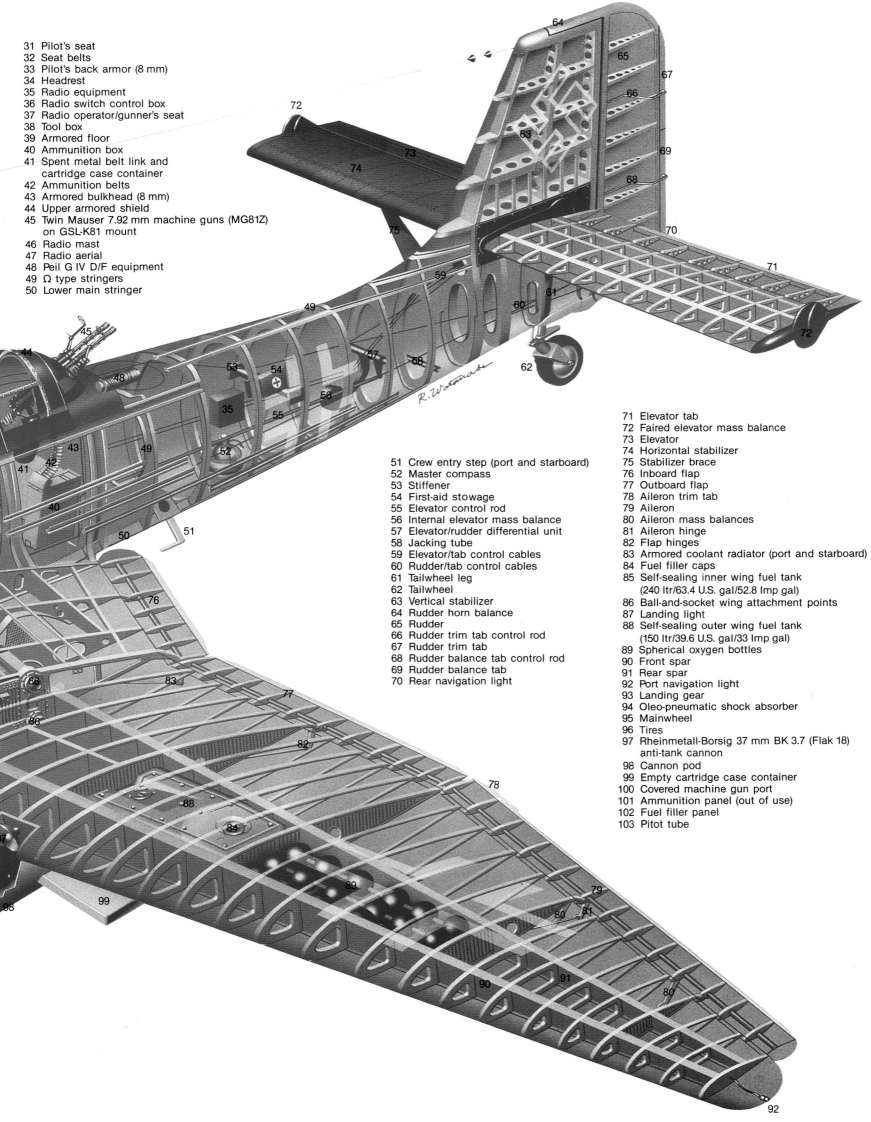

31 Pilot's seat
32 Seat belts
33 Pilot's back armor (8 mm)
34 Headrest
35 Radio equipment
36 Radio switch control box
37 Radio operator/gunner's seat
38 Tool box
39 Armored floor
40 Ammunition box
41 Spent metal belt link and
   cartridge case container
42 Ammunition belts
43 Armored bulkhead (8 mm)
44 Upper armored shield
45 Twin Mauser 7.92 mm machine guns (MG81Z)
   on GSL-K81 mount
46 Radio mast
47 Radio aerial
48 Peil G IV D/F equipment
49 Ω type stringers
50 Lower main stringer

51 Crew entry step (port and starboard)
52 Master compass
53 Stiffener
54 First-aid stowage
55 Elevator control rod
56 Internal elevator mass balance
57 Elevator/rudder differential unit
58 Jacking tube
59 Elevator/tab control cables
60 Rudder/tab control cables
61 Tailwheel leg
62 Tailwheel
63 Vertical stabilizer
64 Rudder horn balance
65 Rudder
66 Rudder trim tab control rod
67 Rudder trim tab
68 Rudder balance tab control rod
69 Rudder balance tab
70 Rear navigation light

71 Elevator tab
72 Faired elevator mass balance
73 Elevator
74 Horizontal stabilizer
75 Stabilizer brace
76 Inboard flap
77 Outboard flap
78 Aileron trim tab
79 Aileron
80 Aileron mass balances
81 Aileron hinge
82 Flap hinges
83 Armored coolant radiator (port and starboard)
84 Fuel filler caps
85 Self-sealing inner wing fuel tank
   (240 ltr/63.4 U.S. gal/52.8 Imp gal)
86 Ball-and-socket wing attachment points
87 Landing light
88 Self-sealing outer wing fuel tank
   (150 ltr/39.6 U.S. gal/33 Imp gal)
89 Spherical oxygen bottles
90 Front spar
91 Rear spar
92 Port navigation light
93 Landing gear
94 Oleo-pneumatic shock absorber
95 Mainwheel
96 Tires
97 Rheinmetall-Borsig 37 mm BK 3.7 (Flak 18)
   anti-tank cannon
98 Cannon pod
99 Empty cartridge case container
100 Covered machine gun port
101 Ammunition panel (out of use)
102 Fuel filler panel
103 Pitot tube

R. Watanabe

winter, the *Luftwaffe* simply did not have enough aircraft and once again had to improvise. The intensity of the fighting at that time is indicated by combat attrition of some of the formations involved: by 22 December 1942 when the unit had to fall back to Voroshilovgrad, II/Sch.G 1 had lost all its Bf109Es, and only seven of its Hs129B-1s were still serviceable. As a temporary measure it was reinforced by the *Panzerjägerstaffel* of JG 51, a union that proved mutually beneficial: the well-trained JG 51 'tank busters' had a good effect on 4/Sch.G 1 personnel, and the JG 51 crews benefitted from a well-established workshop. In late 1942, spare parts for the still relatively 'new' Hs129B were hard to come by. Although this arrangement only lasted a few weeks, both 'tank hunting' units left their mark: between 1 and 16 January 1943 they destroyed 13 tanks each, despite the low daily serviceability rate of only two to three aircraft.

The balance sheet of II/Sch.G 1 for 1942 shows a total of 6,500 sorties (1,532 by Hs129Bs) during which 1,386.5 tons of bombs were dropped. This *Gruppe* claimed 52 Soviet aircraft shot down and 55 destroyed on the ground. With active Hs129B participation, the list of ground targets destroyed is headed by 91 tanks, 1,081 motor vehicles and 273 other vehicles, all at the loss of 20 Hs129B-1s, 16 Bf109Es and three Hs123s.

The appearance of concentrated 'break-through' formations of Soviet tanks during the summer battles of 1942 had spurred a series of anti-tank developments, including proposals by front-line *Luftwaffe* officers to use existing aircraft types as 'carriers' of large-calibre guns for anti-tank use. This had a positive response in *Luftwaffe* command circles, as the Hs129B was not ideal for the task, and its production was rather slow: only 219 Hs129B-1s were delivered in 1942, or about 18 aircraft per month.

Good as these proposals were, the problem in spring 1943 was the lack of larger-calibre cannon suitable for airborne anti-tank use. The first 50 mm BK 5s (modified KwK 39 tank guns) were still undergoing trials, but a solution was soon found. One of the frontline officers who had suggested the use of such weapons, *Oberleutnant* Hans-Ulrich Rudel, proposed the use of the older 37 mm Flak 18 anti-aircraft gun. This weapon was on hand in large numbers, since due to some difficulties with its breech, it had been largely replaced in service by the improved Flak 36. With certain modifications, the Flak 18 could be made into a useful 'flying anti-tank gun'. This proposal was examined and accepted by weapons experts, and the Flak 18, with its barrel shortened and its operation converted to electro-pneumatic firing, became the BK 3.7.

In summer 1942 the first two BK 3.7 cannon were fitted under the wings of a Ju87. Firing trials at the Tarnewitz test centre were highly successful, and the Ju87G anti-tank conversion was declared fit for operational use. In many ways an anachronism, the Ju87G was destined to become the most successful 'flying tank buster' type of World War II.

Other guns suitable for this task were the 30 mm MK 103 (a shorter, lighter and faster-firing development of the MK 101) and the 75 mm Pak 40L, the best anti-tank gun on the Eastern Front. Due to its potential, and the obvious problems involved, experts decided to make use of the biggest weapon. Owing to its size and weight, this gun was fitted into a converted Ju88A-4 bomber airframe, redesignated Ju88PV1 and installed slightly left of centre and inclined 4° downwards. Firing tests began in July 1942. The developed Ju88P-1 version was armed with the proper BK 7.5 with a 12-round magazine. The weapon was enclosed in a large streamlined underfuselage pannier that could be blown off in an emergency. Altogether ten Ju88P-1 conversions were completed late in 1942. However, it was then

Test firing of a 37 mm BK 3.7 fitted to the wings of a Junkers Ju87G-1. (Bundesarchiv)

decided to try them out as 'heavy bomber destroyers' against U.S. Eighth Air Force B-17 heavy day bombers raiding deep into German-occupied Europe: accurate fire against bombers from a safe distance required a large-calibre weapon. Part of the Ju88P series was earmarked for this role, but after some inconclusive encounters and several losses, the remaining Ju88P-2 and P-4 aircraft had to be relegated to the anti-tank role. The only conversion built from the outset exclusively for the anti-tank role was the Ju88P-3. It was similar to the Ju88P-2 but featured better armour protection around the fuselage nose section and engines. Only a small number of these machines were completed.

In the meantime another step had been taken in the evolution of German 'flying tank busters'.

In December 1942, a special *Versuchskommando für Panzerbekämpfung* (Experimental Anti-Tank Detachment) under *Hptm* Hans-Karl Stepp was formed at the Rechlin test centre to try out various large-calibre cannon on different aircraft types to find the best combination. By then, the *Luftwaffe* command had finally decided to organize the 'flying tank busters', and, among other measures taken, on 17 December the existing two *Schlachtgeschwader* received orders outlining their new complement of three *Gruppen* of Fw190s and one *Panzerjägerstaffel* of Hs129Bs.

During the autumn months of 1942 the Henschel works evolved a better armed version of the basic Hs129B as a dedicated 'tank buster'. This involved a series of trials with the MK 103, BK 3.7 and BK 5, all of which were eventually adopted as *Rüstsätze* for this new version, the Hs129B-2, which was a pure 'gun carrier'.

Meanwhile, the Hs129B-1 received a new anti-tank weapon, the 4 kg (8.8 lb) SD 4/HL hollow-charge bombs, which could penetrate all Soviet tanks from above. Later developments were fitted with a rocket motor. There was also the more powerful 9 kg (19.8 lb) SD 9/HL, usually carried in fours in special drop containers.

Production deliveries of the Hs129B-2 began in spring 1943, replacing the Hs129B-1s which were transferred to the Hs129 training and replacement units.

The year 1942 was also notable for other developments which had a direct bearing on the 'tank buster' story.

A new Soviet rocket projectile was introduced, the armour-piercing ROFS-132. It was slightly heavier than the standard RS-132 and had an increased rocket charge for higher velocity. There was also a dramatic increase in Soviet tank production. Output of the T-34 was boosted to 4,414 by the end of June 1942 and another 8,106 by the end of the year, for a total of 12,520 in just 12 months. Soviet tank factories also produced 2,553 KV-1 heavy tanks and 9,372 light tanks. This enormous total of 24,445 tanks not only replaced all losses but also left sufficient surplus for new tank formations, now organised in Tank Corps, and soon in Tank Armies.

The second important development was the Western Allied Lend-Lease deliveries to the Soviet Union, which increased the number of tanks and aircraft. By the end of 1942 these deliveries totalled 4,048 tanks and 3,052 aircraft—more than the German armed forces had at the beginning of Operation Barbarossa. By the end of hostilities in 1945, the U.S. Lend-Lease aid to the Soviet Union alone amounted to 13,303 tanks and 14,798 aircraft besides much other material, none of

SD 4/HL

4 kg (8.8 lb) hollow-charge anti-vehicle/anti-personnel bomb. The bomb body is made of cast iron and screwed on to the nose cap. The tail unit is sheet steel and spot welded together.

Length overall: 310 mm (12.3 in)
Body length: 197 mm (7.75 in)
Body diameter: 90 mm (3.5 in)
Total weight: 4.2 kg (9.25 lb)
Weight of filling: 340 g (0.75 lb)

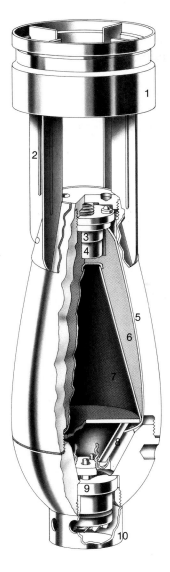

1 Circular strut
2 Tail fin
3 Gaine
4 Terminal
5 Electric leads
6 Cast TNT
7 Shaped charge liner
8 Plastic support
9 Z 66 fuze
10 Fuze retainer ring

which was ever paid for.

The third development was an innovation in anti-tank defence: the *Panzerfaust*. This unique hand-held one-shot rocket-propelled anti-tank weapon was evolved in Germany in 1942 to provide the infantryman with his own anti-tank defence. The hollow-charge warhead could penetrate up to 200 mm of armour, but it had a limited launching range (initially just 30 m/33 yds) and a dangerous rocket flame. Nevertheless, it was a deadly anti-tank weapon and made things more difficult for the attacking tanks. The first 30-metre models appeared on the Eastern Front late in 1942.

In spring 1943 the *Versuchskommando für Panzerbekämpfung* was ordered to Bryansk for operational trials. This experimental detachment had expanded to one *Staffel* each of cannon-armed Ju87G, Hs129B, Ju88P and Bf110G. The Ju87G *Staffel* was led by the newly promoted *Hptm* Rudel. It soon became obvious that the Ju88P and Bf110G were not really suitable for low-level attacks. Even the favoured Ju87G was at first not doing so well: during one of the early trial operations the Ju87G *Staffel* lost several aircraft without achieving any success. What impressed Rudel and the other pilots of his unit was the accuracy of the BK 3.7 cannon: using the ordinary Revi reflex gunsight, it was possible to hit a target as small as 30 × 30 cm (11 ^{13}/$_{16}$ in) at a distance from 100–150 m (110–165 yds). Provided the pilot kept his Ju87G steady, he could hit any vulnerable part of a tank from that distance. Examination of captured Soviet tanks clearly revealed the 'weak spots:' the engine, fuel tanks and ammunition, the location of which varied only slightly from one tank type to another.

T-34 tanks advance towards the front during the Battle of Kursk in July 1943. (TASS)

These operational trials lasted 14 days, and when they concluded, Rudel was ordered by the RLM to take his *Staffel* to the Crimea. The Ju87G were in action just two days after their arrival when the whole *Staffel* was ordered to stop several Soviet tanks dangerously close to its own lines. The order was a mistake; Rudel's Ju87G was hit by Soviet anti-aircraft fire before it had even reached the main combat zone, and his *Staffel* was driven off by strong Soviet defences. During this action the Germans had their first encounter with Soviet-flown Spitfire Mk V fighters, effective evidence of the Lend-Lease.

The lessons were clear: the Ju87G could not be flown against targets near an established main combat zone. The Soviet troops were well supplied with automatic light anti-aircraft guns and used all infantry firearms against low-flying aircraft. Unless involved in a breakthrough operation, Soviet tanks at that time did not move further than 1,000–1,500 m (1,100–1,640 yds) from their own lines and so were protected by their locally deployed light anti-aircraft guns. In short, the Ju87G could only be used successfully when the ground situation was fluid. Otherwise, the only way it could operate was by flying together with Ju87 dive bombers to neutralise some of the anti-aircraft defences.

As the most experienced Ju87 pilot, Rudel was not overenthusiastic. Loaded with two underslung cannon, the Ju87—never a fast aircraft—was slower and could not carry bombs or dive. Added to that, the 12 rounds per gun only allowed two or three firing passes before pilots had to leave the battlefield to reload—unless the pilot was a very good shot. The only benefits were the proven accuracy of the BK 3.7 cannon and the fact that contrary to general opinion the current Ju87D was not such a heavy-handed aircraft as it was made out to be.

Two months later, on 17 June 1943, the Experimental Anti-Tank Detachment was disbanded and the aircraft dispersed. The next few weeks were like the proverbial calm before the storm, still hidden behind the nondescript codename *Unternehmen Zitadelle*, Operation Citadel.

In February 1943 another anti-tank detachment, which was to have an important operational significance, was formed at Khortitsa under *Luftflotte* 4. Known as *Panzerjagdkommando Weiss*, it was commanded by *Major* Otto Weiss, a highly decorated ground-attack pilot and leader who was destined to play a very important role in the evolution of German 'flying tank busters'. From the start, the *Panzerjagdkommando Weiss*, composed of several Hs129 *Staffeln*, achieved some notable successes against incursions of Soviet tanks. One of the more important actions took place during a Soviet breakthrough at the small bend of the Don River when sections of Hs129B-1s from the *Pzjagdkdo Weiss* attacked and set fire to ten

Soviet tanks and recorded observed hits on many more during the two-day battle. Stuka and other bomber formations were also operational in the same area but failed to achieve any success against Soviet armour.

These operations led to the establishment of the new post of *Führer der Panzerjägerstaffel* (Leader of Tank Hunting Flights), which for the first time combined all Hs129B *Staffeln*, hitherto operating separately. This concentration of 'tank hunting' formations under one command soon proved its worth.

Operation Citadel, recorded in military history as the Battle of Kursk, was the last German attempt to destroy the bulk of the Soviet armour and regain the initiative. The Soviet 'balcony' protruding into the German lines was an obvious place for a battle and acted like a magnet on both sides. Thanks to a highly placed German traitor codenamed *'Werther,'* Soviet Intelligence was kept fully informed of the dispositions and strengths of German ground and air formations, enabling the Soviets to make the necessary preparations. When the German forces finally struck early on 5 July 1943, the greatest confrontation of armour ever seen on the field of battle was launched: some 2,600 German tanks (including nearly all available Panthers, Tigers, the latest PzKw IVs and 370 assault guns) and about 3,600 Soviet tanks (predominantly T-34s) and assault guns, all concentrated at a salient no more than 70 km (43 mls) wide at its neck.

By 12 July, after some very hard fighting, the southern German assault group under General Manstein had very nearly succeeded in breaking the last Soviet defensive line when the Soviet command ordered its counterattack north of the Kursk salient, spearheaded by hundreds of T-34s. Combined with the very heavy losses of armour and troops from some of the best German formations and the Western Allied landing in Sicily two days before, this Soviet attack resulted in an immediate halt of the German offensive, and the end of Citadel.

Apart from the premature operational debut of the new German Panther tanks, the Battle of Kursk and its immediate sequel, the Soviet counteroffensive witnessed the debut of several new weapons on the Soviet side, such as the 50-ton SU-152 heavy assault gun based on the KV-1 chassis. In the air, the Battle of Kursk marked the combat debut of the Lavochkin La-5FN fighter-bomber which, in some respects, had a better performance than the contemporary Fw190.

Of more interest to this narrative are the other new Soviet weapons first used in July–August 1943: the small PTAB hollow-charge anti-tank bombs; the Il-2M two-seater armed with two 37 mm wing cannon, used specifically for anti-tank operations; and the Yak-9T fighter fitted with a 37 mm

Ju87G-1 of *Versuchskommando für Panzerbekämpfung* on the Easten front in early summer 1943. (Bundesarchiv)

Loaded with two AB 70D1 containers, a Hs129B-1/R2 of 8(Pz)/Sch.G 2 heads for the target in mid-1943. (Bundesarchiv)

cannon between the engine cylinder blocks for the same purpose.

In this short but ferocious battle of attrition the losses on both sides were high, but as the obviously inflated claims can never be verified, this narrative will only record the highlights of the 'flying tank buster' operations.

On the very first day of *Zitadelle* the counterattacking Soviet armour provided an ideal target for the 'flying tank busters:' the tanks were on the move, the ground anti-aircraft defences were disorganised, and their fighter cover irregular. The first to try his hand was *Hptm* Rudel, who took off with his cannon-armed Ju87G, followed by the whole 1 *Staffel* loaded with bombs. During the very first attack flight four Soviet tanks exploded under the hammer blows of Rudel's 37 mm cannon; by the end of the day his total stood at 12. This score marked the beginning of the amazing 'tank busting' career of this German pilot, a true one-man campaign against armour. The first Ju87G 'tank busting' *Staffel* was born that day, with Rudel in command.

'We tried all kinds of attacks. We would dive on the steel colossus from behind, from the sides. Our gliding angle was not too steep, so as not to take us right down to the ground and avoid the difficulties in levelling off should the machine suddenly stall. If the stall is too deep, there is no chance to avoid hitting the ground, with all the unpleasant results.

We tried to hit the tanks in their weakest spots. The frontal part is always the strongest, and this is why the tanks always try to show their thick foreheads to the enemy whenever possible. It is more vulnerable along the flanks but the best aiming part is the rear where the engine is located covered by thin armour plating. Also, to improve cooling of the engine, this plating has a number of large holes. That is where it pays to hit them, because where there is an engine, there is always fuel!

Along their flanks there are fuel tanks and ammunition, but the armour protection there is thicker than at the back.

It is quite easy to spot a moving tank from the air; the blue engine exhaust smoke is a giveaway.

While *Hptm* Rudel started making a name for himself as a solo 'tank buster' flying the Ju87G, the Hs129B formations also left their mark on the battlefield.

On 5 July 1943 four of the five Hs129B *Staffeln* (4 and 8/Sch.G 1 and 4 and 8/Sch.G 2), which formed the 'flying anti-tank force' deployed for Operation Citadel under the overall command of *Hptm* Bruno Meyer, were based at Mikoyanka. *Hptm* Meyer was an experienced ground support pilot and leader and had been actively involved in the formation of the Hs129 'tank busting' units.

Their call came three days after the start of *Zitadelle* when, during a battlefield reconnaissance flight, Bruno Meyer spotted a Soviet tank brigade assembling west of Byelgorod for a surprise attack on the open flank of the II *SS Panzerkorps*. The following action was an exemplary 'tank busting' operation. Summoning his 'immediate readiness' *Staffel* to attack, *Hptm* Meyer alerted the other three *Staffeln* to follow at spaced intervals. Within minutes, the first 16 Hs129B-1s were on the scene, attacking the assembling T-34s from the flanks and rear and opening fire from about 500 m (550 yds). The second *Staffel* of 16 Hs129B-1s was already approaching the area and took over after the first *Staffel* had used up its ammunition. In the meantime, the third Hs129B-1 *Staffel* was on the way and the fourth taking off as the first was coming in to refuel and rearm.

The operation was a complete success: most of the T-34s were destroyed and the remainder fled. It was a classic case of aircraft achieving a decisive victory on the battlefield without any involvement of the ground forces.

Nearly two weeks later, at the height of the Soviet counteroffensive, the Hs129B *Staffeln* were again instrumental in stopping another Soviet tank brigade from achieving its objective. This tank formation had broken through the lines

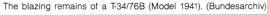

The blazing remains of a T-34/76B (Model 1941). (Bundesarchiv)

A knocked-out KV-1. (Bundesarchiv)

held by the German 9th Army and was racing towards the vital Orel-Karachev rail and road link. Once again, the Hs129Bs succeeded in destroying most of the attacking T-34s and saving the situation without any help from the ground forces.

But the *Luftwaffe* 'tank busters' were not the only ones wreaking death and destruction among the armour during those sweltering July and August days in 1943.

For the defence of the Kursk salient and the planned counterstroke, the Soviet command had concentrated nearly 60 percent of its air power within the framework of four Air Armies. The several hundred *Shturmoviks* available to the Soviet command had at their disposal the new PTAB-2.5-1.5 anti-tank bombs and several regiments of Il-2 *tip* 3M 'tank hunters' armed with 37 mm NS-37 cannon for operational trials.

The small hollow-charge PTAB (*Protivotankovaya Aviatsionnaya Bomba*, anti-tank aviation bomb) were carried in special cassettes fitted inside the Il-2 *tip* 3 wing bomb cells and scattered over German tank concentrations during assembly or on the move. The Il-2 could carry 220 PTAB-2.5-1.5 kg bombs which would cover an area of approximately 3,000 m² (3,600 sq yds). The density was such that even if the 220 bombs were dropped at just one tank, at least one bomb was bound to hit it and burn its way inside. A PTAB-2.5-1.5 bomb hit at 0° could penetrate 60 mm of armour, its explosive wave reaching an intensity of 11,000 m (36,100 ft)/sec. To improve the bombing accuracy, the PBP-1 gunsight, which did not have the full frontal semisphere vision, was replaced by a ring-shaped sight designed by Vasilyev. Attacks with PTAB bombs were claimed to be two to three times more effective than bombing runs with ordinary bombs.

According to Soviet sources, the PTAB-2.5-1.5 kg bombs were used for the first time on 5 July 1943, when 291 ShAD (Assault Aviation Division) claimed the destruction of 30 German tanks. Another recorded use of these small hollow-charge bombs occurred during the Soviet Mius operation on 30 July 1943, when 504 ShAP/1 Guards ShAD caught a column of 70 German tanks preparing for a counterattack. In five consecutive 'attacks from a circle', the Il-2s dropped 1,232 PTAB-2.5-1.5 kg bombs and set fire to 15 German tanks. The average distance between individual PTAB bombs was 60–70 m

(70–80 yds) on the ground. When attacking small groups of tanks, the average hit probability was about 15 percent. The effect on the morale of the German tank crews was much greater, since their only defence in the field was fighter protection, and they were not always available.

As noted earlier, the *Luftwaffe* had introduced small hollow-charge anti-tank bombs the previous year but never seemed to have developed them or exploited their potential despite the dire need for effective anti-tank weapons.

The Il-2 *tip* 3M was an attempt to produce a Soviet cannon-armed 'tank buster'. The 37 mm NS-37 cannon was an original Soviet design incorporating several novel features.

However, this installation was not a success. The 37 mm barrels protruded some distance ahead of the wings, and the whole installation (including 64 rounds of ammunition) made the Il-2 *tip* 3M 760 kg (1,680 lb) heavier than the standard version. Apart from that, the NS-37 was short-recoil operated and, when fired, gave the aircraft a swaying motion, which made it very difficult to fire more than a couple of rounds at the same target. Even more important was the effect of this installation on manoeuverability, which made this cannon-armed 'tank buster' heartily disliked by Il-2 pilots.

Nevertheless, at the time of the Kursk battle in July 1943 the NS-37 had reached the operational-trials stage, and at least two *Shturmovik* regiments were reportedly equipped with the Il-2 *tip* 3M. However, their combat debut is variously reported as 8 July and 20 July. The Il-2 'tank busters' would fly past the advancing German tank column, slightly to one side, then circle around and attack from the rear. After the first firing pass the machines would climb away and bank to attack again. These cannon attacks would last 15–20 minutes. According to Soviet sources, during one such attack the German 9th Panzer Division lost 70 tanks in 20 minutes.

These operational tests lasted until 16 December 1943, but no large scale use of the Il-2 *tip* 3M was ever made. An unknown number of single-seat and two-seat Il-2s were also fitted with the NS-37 cannons by forward maintenance units, and some 'long-barrel' Il-2s are known to have been operational in 1944, but no details of their effectiveness are known.

But that was not quite the end of the Soviet large-

PzKw IV Ausf. Hs and a PzKw III (probably Ausf. M, the second from the right) on the steppe during Operation Citadel in July 1943. (Bundesarchiv)

calibre anti-tank cannon story. In an attempt to create a faster, more manoeuverable 'tank buster' the Soviet military turned to single-seat fighters. The only types suitable for an engine-mounted NS-37 installation late in 1942 were the Yak-9 and LaGG-3, but the latter soon proved too unwieldy. The first Yak-9T (*Tyazholi*=heavy, or *Tankov*=for tanks) appeared in spring 1943. Due to the slow delivery of the NS-37 cannons a number of Yak-9Ts were fitted with alternative, lighter cannons, but no details are known of their operational use.

The Yak-9 was considered such an accommodating aircraft that it was decided to go a step further. The Yak-9K (*Krupnokaliberny*=large-calibre), also developed in 1943, was generally similar to the Yak-9T but armed with the 45 mm OKB-16-45 cannon. It had a magazine capacity of 15 rounds. Only a small number of Yak-9Ks were completed and used operationally—mainly against shipping in the Black Sea. One Yak-9K was even fitted with a slightly modified 57 mm anti-tank cannon, but that was asking too much.

Il-2 tactics had also evolved with combat experience. Instead of quick low-level passes, a squadron of Il-2 *Shturmovik*s would approach their target at about 800–1,200 m (2,620–3,940 ft) altitude in a 'wedge' or *peleng* (staggered line abreast) formation. The attack would start from a shallow dive of 30°–40°, using an attack formation best suited to the nature and the anti-aircraft defences of the target.

Bombs and/or rocket projectiles would be released when 200–300 m (220–330 yds) from the target, followed by repeated passes with cannon and machine gun fire.

All these forms of attack were developed to take advantage of the Il-2's maximum potential. This related especially to German tanks and armoured troops which would be singled out and hunted down by relays of Il-2s. The priorities were the same as before, and there were *Shturmovik*s to spare.

A favourite form of attack, approaching the target from the rear, often ensured surprise, a higher probability of destroyed tanks and other mobile targets and gave the Il-2s a better chance to avoid anti-aircraft defences. The basic rule here was that such targets had to be at least 3–5 km (2–3 mls) from the front lines.

Apart from minor refinements, these tactics remained practically unchanged until the end of the war.

Although by late 1943 the Soviet Air Force had numerical superiority and much improved combat techniques, they never achieved total air superiority on the Eastern Front. The Soviet respect for the *Luftwaffe* was illustrated by the frequent one-for-one fighter escort for the Il-2s. Even so, there

Il-2 *tip* 3M (Il-2m3) in formation flight. (Novosti Press)

were still problems.

On escorted Il-2 raids the fighter leader would take charge of the *Shturmovik*s if their commander was shot down or his radio failed. By this time the *Shturmovik*s penetrated much deeper, 40–60 km into the German-held territory, whereas earlier they seldom ventured further than 6–10 km behind the lines.

No official statistics of *Shturmovik* losses have been published, but a *Luftwaffe* estimate for 1943 claims that 6,900 Il-2s had been shot down. Other attrition due to non-operational causes must also have been quite considerable.

A good share of this large number of Il-2s shot down was due to another new weapon introduced that year: the armoured mobile anti-aircraft gun.

Tanks have had a fear of aircraft from very early days, as demonstrated by the provision of anti-aircraft machine gun fittings on Soviet and German (but not British, French or American) tanks before the start of World War II. However, anti-aircraft machine gun fittings were abandoned by German tanks because mobile anti-aircraft guns always accompanied their armoured formations. Why this form of tank anti-aircraft defence was neglected in Soviet armed forces is not quite clear; their only defence against low-flying aircraft were the quadrupled 7.62 mm Maksim machine guns mounted on trucks. A few experimental self-propelled anti-aircraft guns were produced late in 1942 but this line was not pursued.

On the German side, due to the increasing threat of *Shturmovik* attacks, the *Flakpanzer* had become a necessity in 1942/43. They ranged from the early *Flakpanzer* 38 (2 cm), on a Czech-built PzKw 38(t) chassis, through the much more potent anti-*Shturmovik* weapon, *Flakpanzer* IV, with its four-

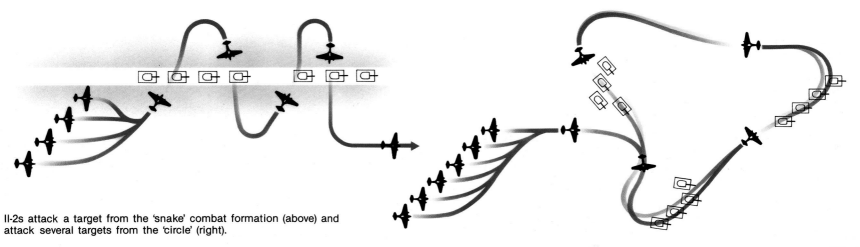
Il-2s attack a target from the 'snake' combat formation (above) and attack several targets from the 'circle' (right).

Two Hs129B-2/R2s of 8(Pz)/Sch.G 2 prepare to take off from an airfield on the Eastern Front in the summer of 1943. (Bundesarchiv)

barrelled 20 mm Flak 38, protected by hinged armour plates, to the more developed *Wirbelwind* with the same armament and the *Ostwind* (37 mm Flak 43) on a PzKw IV chassis. Several other developments remained in prototype stage in 1945.

The Soviet counteroffensive beginning with the Battle of Kursk gradually spread out from Smolensk to the Black Sea and, notwithstanding heavy losses, continued with undiminished force in September and November. The German command now faced a growing 'tank crisis' as groups of mainly T-34s, often supported by regiments of *Shturmoviks* and *'Katyusha'* rocket barrages, kept smashing through the German lines. Static defences, such as guns and dug-out tank traps soon proved insufficient; this was the time of the self-propelled anti-tank guns, the only mobile ground defence that could still master these sudden crisis situations. However, the most mobile anti-tank defence were the aircraft.

Lacking suitable air-to-ground rockets the *Luftwaffe* command put great hopes in the cannon-armed 'tank hunters.' The Ju87G was only a temporary solution; the Stuka had never been intended as a ground attack aircraft, and its chances of survival when used against protected enemy armour were low.

Despite its shortcomings, the Hs129B was the only suitable German aircraft, but little could be done to improve its performance or the reliability of its engines. A faster ground attack/anti-tank aircraft was needed, an aircraft that could look after itself after disposing its offensive load. That aircraft was the Fw190, modified for the ground support role as the Fw190F

Ammunition loading work for the 30 mm MK 103 cannon of an Hs129B-2/R2. (Bundesarchiv)

and G series. However, as the Fw190 was urgently needed by the *Luftwaffe* fighter formations, the planned re-equipment of ground support units could only occur gradually.

By early autumn 1943, each of the *Luftwaffe*'s four *Schlachtgeschwader* had added a 10(Pz) *Staffel* to its establishment, temporarily equipped with Ju87Gs. The long overdue reorganisation and rationalisation of the *Luftwaffe Stuka-* and *Schlachtflieger* formations finally materialised on 1 September 1943. The first *General der Schlachtflieger, Oberst* Dr Ernst Kupfer, lost his life in a flying accident. His successor, *Oberst* Hubertus Hitschhold, another highly decorated Stuka commander, was convinced that both the Hs129B and the Ju87G should be replaced by the Fw190F and G series as quickly as possible. This was fine as far as the ground support went, but was unsatisfactory in the 'tank buster' role. Various Fw190 modifications armed with experimental weapons were still far from the production stage, and the problem remained unresolved.

On 18 October 1943 all former *Stuka-, Schlacht-, Schnellbomber-* and *Panzerjäger* formations were renamed *Schlachtgeschwader* (SG), thus ending the previous profusion of unit designations. From that date, all *Panzerjägerstaffeln* were formed into one unit, IV(*Panzer*)/SG 9 under *Major* Bruno Meyer, although the individual *Staffeln* still remained scattered all along the Eastern Front. They were assisted by some Rumanian-flown Hs129Bs, the only aircraft of this type supplied to one of Germany's allies. The Rumanian unit was the *Grupul* 8 *Assalt* (8 Assault Group) which became operational in 1943 with 62 Hs129B-1/B-2s. It flew many anti-tank sorties on the southern sector of the Eastern Front in cooperation with *Luftflotte* 4 and 6 until autumn 1944.

In the meantime, all former Stuka formations were re-equipped with the Fw190F and G at about two *Gruppen* every six weeks.

The first attempt to create a high-speed 'tank buster' was made late in 1943 with a Fw190F-3 fitted with two 30 mm MK 103 cannon in underwing fairings. It was not a success: due to oscillations when firing the long-barrelled MK 103 proved unsuitable as a wing-mounted weapon; hit dispersal was far too wide for anti-tank operations. Only three Fw190F-3/R3 conversions were completed. However, with the Hs129B phasing out and no other effective airborne anti-tank weapon available, another attempt to convert the Fw190F was made in 1944. The MK 103 cannons were carried in better streamlined fairings and

A Focke-Wulf Fw190F-2 (foreground) fitted with a SC 250 (250 kg/551 lb general purpose) bomb under the fuselage and a Fw190F-3 with four SC 50 (50 kg/110 lb general purpose) bombs beneath the wings in the winter of 1943-44. (Bundesarchiv)

fitted with special barrel supports, but only two Fw190 F-8/R3 conversions were completed in November 1944. By then, various novel rocket-powered anti-tank weapons were under test and seemed to offer a better solution, but these developments had started too late: the Soviet tanks were already on German soil.

The year 1944 was marked by relentless Soviet attacks and German retreats from all occupied territories in the East, except Courland in Latvia. One battle stands out above all others: the Soviet summer offensive. Timed to coincide with the first day of the German attack on the Soviet Union three years before, it struck with ferocity at the German Army Group Centre, which simply disintegrated.

The Hs129 *Panzerjägerstaffeln* were in the thick of the fighting but their efforts were in vain: there were never enough 'tank busters' to cope with the attacking massed tank formations. The attrition rate of Hs129B units had risen to 20 percent, and replacements could no longer keep up with losses.

This period also added more ground ingredients to the 'tank buster' story. The first of these was the T-34/85 tank, an up-gunned and up-armoured development of the basic T-34. It was first encountered on 15 December 1943. The other was the formidable IS (Iosif Stalin) tank armed with a 100 mm and then a 120 mm gun. The IS-2 was first met in battle near Korsun in February 1944. Increasing numbers of these powerful tanks were deployed with Soviet armoured formations and proved very hard nuts to crack, although only a limited number of the even more formidable IS-3 tanks reached the fighting lines before the end of hostilities.

By 1944 the Soviet tanks had become a nightmare to the German command: no matter how many tanks the Germans destroyed, new tank regiments appeared on the battlefield. The skill and daring shown by Soviet tank formation commanders was of the highest order, a complete reversal from the inept handling of only 18 months before.

At this late stage, when the Soviet tanks were literally on the German doorstep, a multitude of ideas and projects on how to deal with this armoured avalanche were put forward.

In the air there was the Hs129B-3/Wa, the final and most powerful version of the series. Airborne firing experiments with the 75 mm BK 7.5 (Pak 40L) had been going on since summer 1942, but its chosen carrier, the Ju88P, was just too large and unwieldy to be a 'flying tank buster'. To assist in these experiments, 11/SG 9 (formerly 8/Sch.G 1) was withdrawn from operations on 20 October 1943, transferred to Udetfeld and

redesignated *Erprobungskommando* 26 (Test Detachment) on 10 January 1944. When the first IS-2 tanks appeared with their 120 mm armour protection, the BK 7.5 became a priority, and another 'carrier' had to be found quickly. There was only one suitable aircraft. In May 1944 a Hs129B was fitted with a wooden mock-up of this large gun and flown to Travemünde for measuring tests. Two months later, the first Hs129B-2/R4s armed with the BK 7.5 cannons underwent hurried firing trials and were then flown straight to the Eastern Front. The relatively small and underpowered aircraft, with its large, heavy long-barrelled anti-tank gun, proved more successful than expected, and the new version, Hs129B-3/Wa, was ordered in production in August. Only 25 machines of this type were built because of the limited supply of BK 7.5 guns then available (30) and the termination of Hs129 production in September 1944 after the completion of 225 aircraft that year (total Hs129B production: 868 aircraft).

The Hs129B-3/Wa,s were delivered to 10 and 14(Pz)/SG 9 and were reportedly very successful against the heavy IS-2 tanks. The BK 7.5 cannons were fitted with a 12-round magazine, and the whole underfuselage pannier could be blown off by explosive charges in an emergency. Because of the destructive effect of its 75 mm gun, the Hs129B gained its descriptive nickname *Büchsenöffner* (Tin opener).

The only attempt to extend the useful life of the Hs129 was a proposed version powered by two 840 hp Isotta-Fraschini RG 17/40 Delta engines. Designated Hs129C, it was to be armed with two 30 mm MK 103 cannon side by side in a remotely controlled ventral barbette, but the aircraft did not advance beyond wind tunnel tests.

It was also at this late stage that German inventors and engineers turned to rocket propulsion for anti-tank missiles fired from aircraft.

As stated earlier, the German military had not been impressed by the Soviet RS-82 aircraft rocket projectiles, and subsequent *Luftwaffe* attempts to use airborne rockets had not been very successful. Against tanks, accuracy and speed were paramount, and the rocket fell short on both. However, by 1944 any weapon was worth a try.

First attempts were adaptations of the standard infantry *Panzerschreck* anti-tank rocket launcher for airborne use. This exigency solution used semi-cylindrical holders for three *Panzerschreck* shells fitted into the ETC bomb racks under each wing of a Fw190F. Firing tests were carried out and the weapon

Fixed Armament of Henschel Hs129

Hs129B-1/R2

1 × 30 mm MK 101 cannon with 30 rounds
2 × 20 mm MG 151/20 cannon with 125 rounds per gun
2 × 7.92 mm MG 17 machine guns with 500 rounds per gun

Rheinmetall-Borsig 30 mm MK 101 cannon
Length: 2,586 mm (101.8 in)
Weight: 139 kg (306 lb)
Muzzle velocity: 700–960 m
                (2,300–3,150 ft)/sec
Rate of fire: 220–260 rounds/min
Armor penetration: 75 mm at 0°
              at 300 m (330 yds)

Hs129B-2/R3

1 × 37 mm BK 3.7 cannon with 12 rounds
2 × 20 mm MG 151/20 cannon with 125 rounds per gun

Rheinmetall-Borsig 37 mm BK 3.7 cannon
Length: 3,626 mm (142.8 in)
Weight: 272 kg (600 lb)
Muzzle velocity: 795–860 m
                (2,610–2,820 ft)/sec
Rate of fire: 140 rounds/min
Armor penetration: 120 mm at 60°
              at 100 m (110 yds)

Hs129B-3/Wa

1 × 75 mm BK 7.5 cannon with 12 rounds
2 × 7.92 mm MG 17 machine guns

Rheinmetall-Borsig 75 mm BK 7.5 cannon
Length: 6,105 mm (240.4 in)
Weight: 705 kg (1,554 lb)
Muzzle velocity: 705 m (2,310 ft)/sec
Rate of fire: 30 rounds/min
Armor penetration: 130 mm at 0°
              at 1,000 m (1,100 yds)

Shells of Anti-Tank Cannon (actual size)

7.92 mm armor
piercing bullet

13 mm armor piercing
incendiary shell

20 mm armor piercing high
explosive self-destroying tracer shell

**75 mm armor piercing tracer
(not self-destroying)**
1 Ballistic cap
2 Cap
3 Projectile body
4 Explosive charge
5 Base fuze
6 Tracer casing

**30 mm armor piercing explosive
incendiary with day tracer**
1 Cap
2 Armor piercing body
3 Incendiary element
4 Explosive element
5 Detonator
6 Fuze

**37 mm high explosive self-
destroying tracer**
1 Fuze
2 Cardboard ring
3 Delay detonator
4 Explosive charge
5 Tracer casing

M. Fg.k.

Mgr

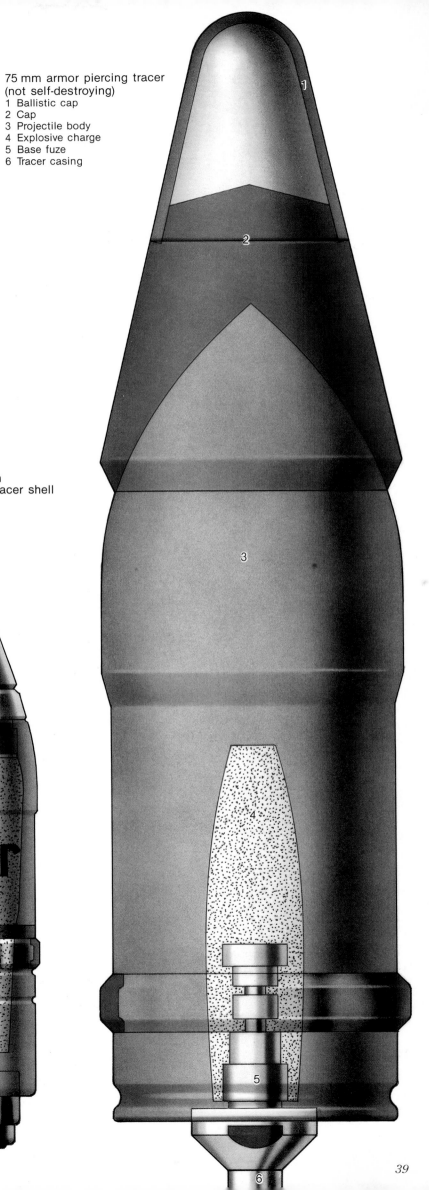

The 'Kanonenvogel' (cannon-armed bird) Ju87G-2, converted from a D-5, taking off on a sortie against Soviet armor in the summer of 1944. (Bundesarchiv)

was used operationally in Hungary in October 1944, but the ballistics were poor and few aircraft were so equipped.

The *Panzerschreck* II made use of the older type 88 mm *Panzerschreck* shells which were more readily available. These were used in two forms: either attached to individual rails fitted four to eight under the wings of a Fw190F, or by a make-shift adaptation of the infantry weapon together with its launching tubes. Some Fw190F-8 ground attack aircraft carried four such tubes under each wing. Tested at Udetfeld, these launchers were also first used operationally on the Eastern Front in October 1944. Their hollow-charge shells had an effective range of 100–120 m (110–130 yds) and could penetrate up to 120 mm of armour.

These make-shift weapons led to the more effective *Panzerblitz* series, only a small number of which reached operational status. There were three progressive versions of this weapon. The original *Panzerblitz* I was abandoned but the *Panzerblitz* II (Pb II) was more promising, comprising the new R4/M fighter rocket fitted with a large hollow-charge warhead. The idea is attributed to *Oberst* Hitschhold, the General of Ground Support Aviation in June 1944. This weapon was so important that *Oberst* Hitschhold personally supervised its installation on Fw190F ground attack aircraft and the training of pilots in its use at Udetfeld, beginning late July 1944. These anti-tank rockets were carried in special metal frames containing six shells each. The Pb II could be fired in salvoes of three, six, nine or the full complement of 12. The drawback was that this framework, nicknamed *Gartenzaun* (Garden fence), could not be jettisoned, and in case of 'stuck' rockets the pilot had to land with them aboard. Aiming was by means of the Revi gunsight, pre-set to compensate for the 2° inclination of the launcher. The accuracy range was 500 m (550 yds) or less; penetration, about 110 mm of armour plate. However, the rocket velocity was again too low, and only a small number of Pb IIs were produced. They were issued to I(Pz)/SG 9, formed in January 1945. Its three *Staffeln* of Fw190F-8 ground attack aircraft were intermittently operational for five to six weeks before lack of fuel curtailed flying.

The Pb III was another adaptation of the R4/M rocket fitted with an even larger hollow-charge warhead. The projectile itself was known as R4/HL and was developed under the highest RLM priority rating. With its increased velocity, the Pb III could penetrate 160 mm of armour at 0° impact. However, only a few of these rockets were produced late in 1944, and none were used operationally.

The most novel anti-tank weapon development was the SG 113A *Förstersonde* (Forester's probe). Basically, this advanced recoilless anti-tank device consisted of vertically mounted shells inside a streamlined container fired by a magnetic probe triggered by a metallic object directly underneath the aircraft. This reaction was instantaneous, and the aircraft could fly at high speed. At the moment of firing an equal balance weight was discharged upwards.

The first air firing trials were carried out early in 1944 with such launchers mounted on several Do17 and Fw189 test aircraft. The initial results were disappointing, but the problems were gradually overcome by using improved electro-magnetic amplifiers. A six-barrelled *Förstersonde* was then fitted into the rear fuselage of a Hs129B-2 for further firing tests. Unfortunately any object on the ground that was higher than the target (such as trees or houses) would trigger off the charges, and the hit probability was as low as 50 percent. During 1944 another two Hs129B-2 and one Fw190F-8 aircraft were equipped with the SG 113A for further firing trials with these 45 mm shells. On the Fw190, three SG 113A barrels were fitted in line inside a flat streamlined fairing mounted vertically into each wing root, projecting above and below the wing surface. On the Hs129B-2 the unit consisted of six SG 113A barrels inside an oval-shaped vertical container behind the pilot's cockpit.

The final series of firing tests carried out at Volkenrode on 18 January 1945 gave more promising results. Two tanks were used as targets, a PzKw V Panther and a captured T-34. The Panther (turret top armour 17 mm) and the T-34 (turret top armour 30 mm) were both hit from a low-level high-speed flight, and the SG 113A shells easily penetrated the turret top armour. A short while later, a captured American M4A3 Sherman tank was used for firing trials at Rechlin, and the SG 113A shells could just about penetrate the 48 mm turret top armour.

To compensate for the high aircraft speed, the SG 113A barrels were inclined 8° backwards. These final trials gave a hit probability of 85–90 percent if the target was on open ground and the attack height did not exceed nine metres.

Special search devices, intended to detect camouflaged tanks, were also under development but remained in the experimental stage, as did several new anti-tank rockets.

By autumn 1944, when most of the existing *Schlachtgeschwader* had already converted to the Fw190F ground attack fighters, *Major* Rudel and some of the crews of III/SG 2 were still flying the cannon-armed Ju87G. Eventually all SG 2 pilots were retrained on their new mounts late in 1944, but Rudel and a group of 'tank sharpshooters' retained their Ju87 'Gustavs' till the end. Shot down for the 30th time on 9 February 1945 while attacking his 13th tank that day, Rudel had to have his leg amputated. He later escaped from the hospital and managed to continue flying with an artificial leg. During the last few weeks of the war Rudel increased his personal score to 519 tanks, equal to five average Soviet tank brigades.

Apart from Hans-Ulrich Rudel there were several other German 'tank buster' pilots with quite respectable scores. The more outstanding were *Lt.d.R.* Anton Korol of 10(Pz)/SG 2 (99 Soviet tanks by 12 March 1945; never shot down or even hit by enemy fire); *Oblt* Wilhelm Joswig of SG 2 (88 Soviet tanks by 29 February 1944; total of 819 operational sorties); *Ofw* Siegfried Fischer of SG 1 (80+ Soviet tanks, many with a rocket-armed Fw190F-8); and *Hptm* Rudolf Ruffer of 10(Pz)/SG 9 (70 Soviet tanks with Hs129B by July 1944; killed in action 16 July 1944). At least 18 known German 'tank buster' pilots destroyed more than 25 Soviet tanks each, but only ten of them survived the war. In many other cases the final score of those killed in action is unknown. There were many others who never returned from their first 'tank hunting' flight.

The last *Schlachtflieger* unit formed by the *Luftwaffe* was the I(Pz)/SG 9, established on 7 January 1945. It incorporated the *Pzjagdstaffel* of SG 1 and 12(Pz)/SG 9. Theoretically, on that date the *Luftwaffe* disposed of seven *Panzerjagdstaffeln*: five under IV(Pz)/SG 9 and two under the newly-formed I(Pz)/SG 9—in addition to *Oberst* Rudel's 10 (Pz)/SG 2—but these unit designations were misleading. Some of the *Staffeln* had only a few aircraft left, and by that time there were hardly any replacements.

There were also some rather odd German 'flying tank busters'. In late autumn 1944, when the 'big anti-tank gun' programme was well advanced, the *Luftwaffe* impressed four Ju288B and C series prototypes, the intended replacement for the He111 which never got past the prototype stage. These four were the only survivors of some 21 machines built when the programme was finally cancelled in summer 1944. They were fitted with the same ventral panneir as the Ju88P-4, armed with a BK 5 cannon, and sent off to join the other big Junkers 'tank busters' in the East.

The other known 'flying tank buster' oddity was even better: the Bücker Bü181 *Bestmann* low-wing trainer fitted with four *Panzerfaust* 100 one-shot infantry anti-tank rocket launchers, two above and two below its wings. Its origins can no longer be ascertained, but the first firing trials with this combination were carried out in mid-March 1945 at Trebbin, just outside Berlin. Attacks were to be flown at very low level, pulling up to 20–30 m (70–100 ft) about 500 m (550 yds) from the target, then going into a shallow dive. The *Panzerfausten* were to be released at about 150–200 m (160–220 yds) from the target,

Petlyakov Pe-2s flying a routine mission in June 1944. (TASS)

followed by an immediate steep evasive turn before the rocket hit the tank.

By 6 April sufficient cadres had been trained to form three units, the 1, 2 and 3 *Panzerjägerstaffeln*. It is no longer clear if all three were in fact formed, but the 3 *Pzjägerstaffel* definitely was, at Kaufbeuren. This unit had 12 Bü181s armed with *Panzerfaust* 100 rockets, but instead of attacking Soviet tanks they were used in dawn and dusk raids on American motorised columns near Tübingen. The *Staffel* was disbanded on 4 May, four days before the end. However, reports still persist that some Bü181s were also used against Soviet tanks near Berlin late in April 1945.

No doubt the most exotic 'tank buster' project at that time would have been the Henschel Hs132 jet-powered ground support aircraft. Three versions were planned, two of which were to be armed with eight *Panzerblitz* II rockets attached to underwing rails in addition to their fixed armament, but this idea was dropped when the Pb II was cancelled.

By late 1944 the Soviet *Shturmoviks* finally had the field to themselves as interference from *Luftwaffe* fighters was minimal, and the Il-2s could attack their targets almost at will. By then, the remaining German tanks and self-propelled guns in the East were having a very hard time and a short life: if they were not spotted and attacked with 123 mm armour-piercing rockets by Il-2s, they were hunted down by Pe-2 dive bombers. By early 1945 a number of Pe-2 pilots had perfected their dive bombing technique to a fine art and were so accurate they could hit practically any target down to the size of a small tank.

The Pe-2s were also fast enough to evade the few intercepting *Luftwaffe* fighters, while most of the Flak guns were involved in ground fighting.

In February 1945 the final *Shturmovik* version to participate in World War II appeared over Eastern Germany—the Il-10. The family likeness was evident except that it was slightly smaller and more streamlined than its predecessor. Powered by an 2,000 hp Mikulin AM-42 engine, the Il-10 was designed from the outset to take an alternative wing armament of two 37 mm NS-37 or two 23 mm VYa cannon, but there is no record of the 37 mm cannon-armed Il-10s being used against German armour.

Fighting in the East officially ended on 8 May 1945, except for Courland in Latvia where the German and most Latvian troops surrendered a day later.

In the end, the tank, assisted by the armoured assault aircraft, won the contest in the East but at a very high price.

The situation was quite different in the West where it was primarily the aircraft that defeated the German armoured forces.

Anti-Tank Weapons for Focke-Wulf Fw190

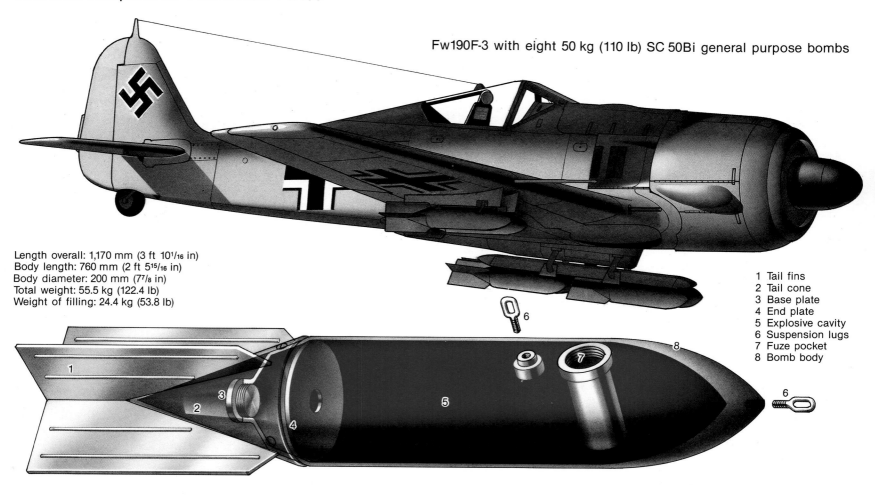

Fw190F-3 with eight 50 kg (110 lb) SC 50Bi general purpose bombs

Length overall: 1,170 mm (3 ft 10$\frac{1}{16}$ in)
Body length: 760 mm (2 ft 5$\frac{15}{16}$ in)
Body diameter: 200 mm (7$\frac{7}{8}$ in)
Total weight: 55.5 kg (122.4 lb)
Weight of filling: 24.4 kg (53.8 lb)

1 Tail fins
2 Tail cone
3 Base plate
4 End plate
5 Explosive cavity
6 Suspension lugs
7 Fuze pocket
8 Bomb body

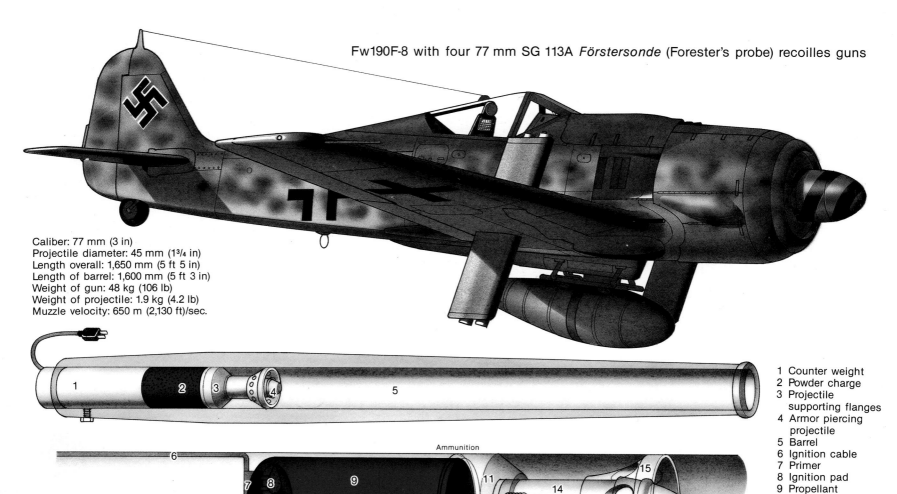

Fw190F-8 with four 77 mm SG 113A *Förstersonde* (Forester's probe) recoilles guns

Caliber: 77 mm (3 in)
Projectile diameter: 45 mm (1$\frac{3}{4}$ in)
Length overall: 1,650 mm (5 ft 5 in)
Length of barrel: 1,600 mm (5 ft 3 in)
Weight of gun: 48 kg (106 lb)
Weight of projectile: 1.9 kg (4.2 lb)
Muzzle velocity: 650 m (2,130 ft)/sec.

Ammunition

1 Counter weight
2 Powder charge
3 Projectile
  supporting flanges
4 Armor piercing
  projectile
5 Barrel
6 Ignition cable
7 Primer
8 Ignition pad
9 Propellant
10 Staff
11 Sabot
12 Fuze
13 Explosive charge
14 Armor core
15 Leading flange

Fw190F-8 with four 28 cm Wfk. Spr. *(Wulfköper Sprengladung)* rockets

Diameter: 280 mm (11 in)
Length overall: 1,190 mm (3 ft 10⁷/₈ in)
Total weight: 82 kg (181 lb)
Weight of explosive filling: 36 kg (79 lb)
Muzzle velocity: 145 m (476 ft)/sec
Range: 750–1,925 m (820–2,105 yds)
Most effective range: 1,000 m (1,090 yds)

1 Wgr. Z50+ fuze
2 Gaine
3 High explosive filling
4 Igniter pad
5 Propellant powder
6 Black powder
7 Venturi
8 Electric igniter

Fw190F-8 with twelve 8 cm Pb 1 *(Panzerblitz 1)* rockets

Diameter: 80 mm (3¹/₈ in)
Length overall: 700 mm (2 ft 3⁹/₁₆ in)
Total weight: 6.9 kg (15.2 lb)
Weight of explosive filling: 0.61 kg (1.34 lb)
Muzzle velocity: 370 m (1,214 ft)/sec.

1 Copper disk
2 Detonator
3 High explosive filling
4 Explosive pellets
5 Thermal arming device
6 Black powder igniter
7 Suspension studs
8 Propellant
9 Primer unit
10 Venturi
11 Closing disk
12 Tail fins

Tank busters over Western Europe

The conditions governing the use of armour and anti-tank weapons, including 'tank busters' in Western Europe (and Normandy in particular) were quite different from those on the Eastern Front.

Apart from their numerical and material superiority, the Western Allies had two other decisive advantages: practically complete aerial supremacy over the battlefield and the rear areas, and Ultra, an amazingly complex and successful code-breaking operation that was eventually able to provide the Allies with increasingly more detailed knowledge of German dispositions and plans.

By early 1944, practically all German radio traffic was recorded and, more often than not, decrypted. The information was then analysed and disseminated via the SLUs (Special Liaison Units) to a small number of authorised recipients from the British Prime Minister and the American President downwards.

It was during the uphill Italian campaign that the Allies decided to leave all ground support and battlefield interdiction to fighter-bombers, evolved the techniques later used in Western Europe and introduced the Republic P-47D Thunderbolt fighter-bomber.

Designed in 1939/40 as an interceptor by Alexander Kartveli, an emigre from Soviet Georgia, the P-47 excelled in altitude performance and diving speed, and it was in Italy, where for lack of aerial targets the Allied air forces had to use fighters for ground support tasks, that the P-47 was to establish itself in that role. In fact, the single-seat P-47D could carry practically the same bomb load as an average twin-engined bomber, reverting to its basic fighter role immediately after bombing. Its rugged structure and the comparatively low degree of vulnerability of its Pratt & Whitney R-2800 radial engine ensured its success as a ground attack aircraft.

Of more importance for the 'tank busting' side of fighter-bomber operations was the evolution of effective dive bombing methods with the P-47D in Italy, where pilots varied the angle of dive according to the target. A steep 60°+ dive was found best for smaller targets, such as tanks, and soon put to widespread use in Normandy.

These, then, were the most important innovations in Allied ground support (and therefore also anti-armour) methods and tactics first used in Italy—and only possible under conditions of aerial and material superiority. The Western Allies had every intention of carrying out their next and biggest operation in Europe under even more favourable conditions.

The decision to rely on fighter-bombers for ground support and the gradual introduction of the aircraft rocket projectile in operational service resulted in diminishing official interest in the development of other aircraft projected specifically for these tasks, including those intended for the anti-tank role. This also applied to the large-calibre aircraft cannon for ground attack use.

The threat of the well-protected German Tiger tanks, not to mention the rather costly experience with RAF No. 6 Squadron in North Africa, caused the idea of using large-calibre aircraft cannon against tanks and other ground targets in Europe to be quietly dropped.

But the large-calibre aircraft cannon still had their supporters in the USA, banking on the 75 mm M4 and AN-M5, although following the promising results shown by indigenous aircraft rockets in 1943 the planned use of large-calibre cannon against armour was changed to anti-shipping operations.

The only other large-calibre American aircraft cannon were the 37 mm M4, M9 and M10. Of these the M9 was specifically designed for use against mechanised forces. However, as far as can be ascertained it was never used against German armour. The later M10 was designed to use the disintegrating link belt feed and had a cyclic rate of fire of 165–170 rpm. It was installed on the Bell P-63 Kingcobra, most of which were sent as Lend-Lease material to the Soviet Union and used in the ground attack/anti-tank role on the Eastern Front.

No specialised ground attack aircraft were evolved in Britain and for the coming invasion of the Continent the air-to-ground rocket projectile was to be the main RAF ground support and anti-tank weapon.

As mentioned in Chapter 2 'Tank busters over the desert', the first RAF rocket-carrying aircraft used against ground targets were an experimental section of Hurricane fighter-bombers despatched post-haste to Tunisia in spring 1943 to counter the German PzKw VI Tiger tanks.

The most important lessons learned from this action were that the 25 lb (11.3 kg) armour-piercing rocket projectile was nowhere near as effective against tanks as the larger 60 lb (27 kg) high-explosive warhead.

The first RAF rocket-carrier intended for use against ground targets on a regular basis was the Hawker Hurricane IV. While it served in that role for some time, it was soon overshadowed by another RAF aircraft that was destined to become the greatest 'rocketeer' of them all, the Hawker Typhoon.

Originally designed in 1937 by Sidney Camm as a potential Spitfire/Hurricane replacement, the Typhoon was rushed into operational service in 1941 before its various inherent faults had been eradicated. By 1943 the Typhoon had found a more rewarding role as a fighter-bomber, although problems with its Napier Sabre sleeve-valve engine and the seepage of carbon monoxide gas into the cockpit were to persist throughout its service life. However, the Typhoon had an unsurpassed acceleration, was very fast at low altitudes, carried a powerful built-in armament and proved able to lift substantial bomb loads. Without anybody realising it, the next step would finally

Hawker Typhoon Mk IB in flight. (Imperial War Museum)

60 lb HE rocket warhead
1 Explosive charge (14 lb/6.4 kg TNT)
2 Fuse   3 Spigot

give the Typhoon the weapon that would reserve it a place in history: the rocket projectile.

The Typhoon's rocket-firing days began in summer 1943 with demonstrations by rocket-armed Hurricane IV fighter-bombers to several squadrons selected for 'rocketeering' operations.

Trials with Typhoons armed with four 60 lb RPs on underwing racks began soon afterwards, and it was then that the pilots began to appreciate some of the more positive points of this new fighter-bomber. The Typhoon, already known as a good gun platform, took to the RPs with ease and could hold its dive without swinging. What the pilot had to watch was his safe pull-out altitude; the Typhoon accelerated and built up speed very rapidly.

Although the British aircraft rocket projectiles had been around since 1941 when they were adopted by the RAF Coastal Command for anti-submarine use, there were no official guidelines regarding their use against ground targets, and operational pilots had to evolve their own tactics. The first operation over German-occupied Europe by No. 181 Squadron on 25 October 1943 against a power station near Caen was a disaster; only the last three of the six attacking Typhoons came back. The lesson was obvious: the practised 30° dive from about 2,000 ft (610 m) was far too shallow and too low for the Typhoons to avoid the light German Flak. Other squadrons went through similar experiences before evolving more suitable tactics—generally a steeper 60° dive, combined with cannon fire to neutralise some of the Flak.

Two other important ingredients of rocket-firing operations were also still being evolved: proper lightweight launchers and a sight.

The early 'rocket carriers' were attached to heavy metal plates fitted flush under the wings to prevent them from being scorched by the rocket exhausts. The excess weight problem was eventually solved by improving the cordite mixture in the rocket motor to cut down the flame, allowing a much thinner gauge plate to be fitted. Attached under them were four pairs of tubular rails, and each rias RP carried by its 'saddles' on a pair of rails. This launcher was known as Rocket Projector Mk I.

The RPs available at that time did not differ much from those evolved late in 1942 and comprised the following:

25 lb AP or SAP (Semi-Armour Piercing) With solid steel warheads, these RPs were designed for use against tanks, submarines, locomotives and similar targets. Under optimum conditions, these RPs could penetrate up to 100 mm of armour. Their maximum speed of 1,580 ft (480 m)/sec was attained in 1 1/2 secs, by which time the RP had travelled 500 yds (460 m). However, these anti-tank RPs did not prove themselves on operations, but they were soon found to be ideal weapons against shipping targets. Contrary to the 60 lb RPs they were very stable under water.

60 lb SAP or HE In this case the warhead consisted of 14 lb (6.4 kg) of TNT filling, and it was initially fitted with a delay fuze. These larger RPs were originally intended for anti-shipping use, the idea being that the warhead would travel 5–15 ft (1.5–4.6 m) inside the hull before exploding. Operational trials were disappointing; the 60 lb warhead had very poor underwater trajectory and was completely useless against submarines.

On the other hand, it proved an ideal weapon against tanks and other armoured targets, thus completely reversing the intended roles of these two RPs.

The third RP was the 25 lb Practice Shot with a concrete warhead.

All three RPs were electrically fired, and the forward pull sheared the individual safety wires that activated small electric igniters placed in front of each cordite charge, which burned from the warhead backwards for better ballistics. The process created a potential danger: the armourers handling the RPs and this vital wiring-up were often given only perfunctory training and there were several bad accidents during the early stages. Eventually the circuits were wired through a multiple socket fitted under the wings, which was 'shorted' by a special plug just before takeoff.

The RPs could be fired either in pairs or salvoes, each Typhoon having a small switch in the cockpit marked accordingly. After selection, the pilot pressed a pushbutton on the throttle lever: once for all eight RPs in a salvo, or four times for four pairs.

As the RPs had quite different trajectories from cannon shells and were affected not only by wind but also by any movement of the aircraft, such as skidding or yawing, pilots had to learn to hold their aircraft absolutely steady when releasing their RPs—and this was where the inherent steadiness of the Typhoon really paid dividends.

Sighting and harmonisation of the RPs were essential and directly related to each other. After various experiments it was found that the standard Mk II pilot's reflector sight fitted with an adjustable screen was the most efficient. This sight was known as Mk IIL.

The graticule range was the usual 100 mph (160 km/h) ring of 6° 11′ angular diameter with a central dot and adjustable range bars.

Harmonising was largely a matter of careful adjustment of launching rails, because the slightest shift immediately diverted the RP at the moment of launching. An error of just $^1/_2$° in the direction of sight could produce an error of nearly 15 ft (4.6 m) when firing at 600 yds (550 m) range—sufficient to miss a small target such as a tank.

In autumn 1942, following the increasing use of aircraft rocket projectiles by the Soviet Air Force and their introduction in RAF service, the U.S. Army Air Force's Ordnance Department began experiments with standard infantry 'Bazooka'-type anti-tank rocket launchers. Firing tests at Wright Field were quite successful and helped to evolve the 4.5 in (114 mm) RP which became the standard American aircraft rocket. Operational suitability tests of this weapon in conjunction with fighter aircraft were ordered by General Henry H. Arnold in September 1943 and were to last over four months. The 4.5 in RP weighed 37 lb (16.8 kg), had an explosive filling of 5 lb (2.3 kg), a launching speed of 800–850 ft (240–260 m)/sec and a range of 4,600 yds (4,200 m). They were launched from 3-tube clusters fitted for trials to all five operational American fighter types—the P-38G, P-39N, P-40E, P-47C and A-36A (P-51 attack version). The original 'Bazooka'-type metal launching tubes, found very cumbersome during trials, were soon replaced by lightweight tubes made of flameproof plastic (M-10) or magnesium compounds (M-15). Two such 3-tube clusters loaded with 4.5 in M-8 or M-10 rocket projectiles weighed 450 lb (204 kg). The final report of these tests is dated 28 February 1944 and states that this type of RP and launcher combination could be used for frontal attacks against area targets but was not suitable for use against point targets, such as tanks. Also, that overall dispersion was so variable it was impossible to compile a dispersion chart. Despite this negative aspect, the M-10 hollow-charge rocket projectiles were theoretically very effective against tanks and other armoured fighting vehicles—and were the only such RPs in the American arsenal.

By then, the most suitable fighter types had also been narrowed down, and thanks to its inherent stability and rugged construction the P-47 was a clear favourite. In December 1943 several P-47Ds at Wright Field were also fitted with slightly modified British Mk I railed launchers; their installation and firing trials were supervised by RAF personnel. These served as prototypes for the later American railed RP launchers.

As on the RAF aircraft, harmonisation of the rocket-armed P-47s was a matter of aligning the launcher tubes (or, later, the rails) with the wing guns. The pilot used his normal Mk VIII gunsight for both weapons.

Although at various times between December 1943 and July 1944 there were seven different P-47D-equipped groups in Italy, none of them used RPs during that period. Later in 1944, several combinations of 'Bazooka'-type and other American aircraft rocket projectiles were carried by P-47Ds based in Italy. They were joined in late spring 1945 by Mustang IVs (P-51D/K) of No. 260 Squadron, RAF. However, from late 1944 onwards there were very few German tanks still operational in Italy and most of these RP sorties were flown against other

A pilot puts his hand on 4.5 in (114 mm) M-10 rocket tubes fitted to a P-47D. Note the 30 combat missions indicated on the fuselage. (USAF)

ground and shipping targets.

The Western Allied aircraft rocket projectile 'tank busting' arena opened in Normandy in June 1944.

Codenamed Operation Overlord, the Allied assault on the Atlantic coastline of France was an enormous undertaking, with air power, and particularly air-to-ground cooperation, planned on a scale never before attempted. Even the Allied strategic air forces were earmarked for tactical operations if need be, overruling the objections of their commanders.

Next to the recently discovered German 'secret weapon' sites, the most important reasons for the assault the half a dozen German tank divisions in Northern France and the presence there of several experienced tank formation commanders, including Field Marshal Rommel. Every effort had to be made to block or hold up German armour during the first few days after the Allied landing. After that, the Allied air forces would join the ground combat in a planned, determined effort to destroy or disable German tanks before they reached the Allied lines. That was to be achieved by two specially assembled air formations, the British 2nd Tactical Air Force, or 2 TAF, commanded by Air Marshal Arthur Coningham, and the American Ninth Air Force, commanded by Brig Gen Lewis Hyde Brereton.

Typhoon fighter-bombers were the mainstay of 2 TAF in the ground support role. The aircraft were combined in several Wings and organised into Nos. 83 and 84 Composite Groups. For a while, it was intended to create 'universal' ground attack units and, in training, emphasis was put on interchangeability of Typhoon RP and bombing equipment so that pilots could switch from one type of target to another on short notice.

However, the conversion times clocked during the first tests in November 1943 were longer than expected, even taking into consideration the use of rocket rails. As flexibility of the relatively limited number of RAF ground support aircraft during the coming operation was of paramount importance, more tests were ordered as a matter of urgency. By the end of 1943 the Hawker plant at Langley had produced new RP rails known as Mk III RP Beams, which after passing the necessary tests, were to be put in production in April 1944.

On D-Day a total of 20 Typhoon squadrons were available; 18 were allocated to 2 TAF and two were kept back in the UK for defensive tasks, but only temporarily. The 18

Four 60 lb (27 kg) rocket projectiles under the starboard wing of a Typhoon Mk IB, which belongs to No. 609 Squadron, 123 Wing. (Imperial War Museum)

Typhoon squadrons formed the backbone of 2 TAF ground support force and most were organised into 'mobile RP Wings'.

The American Ninth Air Force had originally operated in North Africa and Italy and was re-established in the UK in October 1943. The buildup of this tactical formation was without parallel, and in just seven months the Ninth AF had grown to six times the size it had been in North Africa in spring 1943.

While this expansion was taking place, the Ninth participated in Operations Point-blank and Noball, as well as flying many bomber escort sorties. These activities continued right up to May 1944, by which time it was already too late to carry out combined exercises with U.S. troops. As a result, the American assault troops remained almost totally untrained in ground-to-air cooperation, while the Ninth AF fighter-bomber pilots went into action on D-Day without any real experience in ground support. The necessary tactics had to be acquired and assimilated practically on the spot, but the Ninth AF was fortunate in having some gifted and energetic commanders.

Of the 18 fighter groups under the Ninth AF on 5 June 1944 no less than 13 were equipped with the P-47 Thunderbolt, by then already established as the most powerful contemporary American fighter-bomber.

As noted before, the aircraft RPs had already been generally accepted by the Western Allies as the most effective anti-tank weapon in 1943, but subsequent development had diverged. Whereas the Americans preferred complete rounds (ie rocket motor and warhead in one casing) the British, by force of circumstances, had adapted the existing 3 in (76.2 mm) AA rocket, fitting it with different warheads. The British arrangement of using launcher rails had obvious advantages and was also preferred by the American tactical air commanders, but the matter was still unresolved as late as mid-February 1944, less than four months from the planned invasion.

On 24 March 1944, another important decision regarding the use of RPs was made. By then, reality had caught up with theory, and the idea of attempting to create a 'universal attack aircraft' out of the Typhoon foundered on the human element. In the time available, their pilots could not be adequately trained to be good at 'rocketeering', as fighter-bombers, ground strafers and smoke screen layers (as originally envisaged), in addition to looking after themselves as fighters. These require-

ments could only be solved by specialising, selecting a number of squadrons to be trained in each role.

It was decided to start intensive training of RP Typhoon pilots within the next two weeks, which was also the target date for re-equipping the selected Typhoon squadrons. In fact training would cause the most headaches; as late as May the average rocket-firing scores were below 50 percent, with many Typhoon pilots unable to grasp the intricacies of their new weapon. This situation was exacerbated by a lack of instructional material. The first booklet explaining the basic principles of RP firing was not prepared by the Ministry of Aircraft Production until 14 June 1944, eight days after the invasion, and then it remained in draft stage for several weeks.

On 5 May 1944, exactly one month before the planned date of D-Day, the Ninth AF started trials using P-47s fitted with the experimental Mk V rocket projectors. This jettisonable installation attached to standard bomb carriers and could take four M-8 or M-10 RPs on each carrier. However, little time remained to carry out proper trials, standardise fittings or train the pilots, and consequently no Ninth AF P-47Ds carried RPs on D-Day.

According to Allied Intelligence reports of 3 June 1944, the 70 km (43 mls) section of the French coast selected for the Allied invasion of German-occupied Europe was defended by about nine German divisions (some 'incomplete'), increased on D+2 to 13 (five of which would be 'Panzer type') and on D+7 to 27 (nine of which would be 'Panzer type'). It was added that all German Panzer divisions in France were below strength, except the *Panzer Lehr Division* and the 12 *Waffen-SS Panzer Division 'Hitler Jugend'*.

The only important new armoured fighting vehicle introduced in the German armed forces in spring 1944 was the Tiger II or *Königstiger* (King Tiger) heavy tank. A logical development of the Tiger I, the PzKw VI Model B was projected in autumn 1942 and designed for both defensive warfare or the penetration of strong lines of defence. Apart from its larger size, it differed from the Tiger I in having a well-sloped hull armour of increased thickness. Its most prominent feature was the 88 mm KwK 43 L/71 tank gun of exceptional performance.

The *Luftwaffe* in the West was a shadow of its former self, and that fact was well known to the Allies. Despite the long-standing threat of an invasion, the *Luftflotte* 3 was not equipped to meet it. On the eve of D-Day it had 815 aircraft dispersed between Holland and southern France while the Allies had concentrated 10,520 combat aircraft against Normandy alone.

Despite much confusion and many initial setbacks, the invasion was a success and the buildup of Allied forces went ahead more or less as planned. The British landing zone being opposite tank country, the original intention was to take the ancient town of Caen on the first day—and this is where things started to go wrong.

By early morning on D-Day forward units of the British 3 Division suddenly ran into elements of the German 21 Panzer Division, which they had assumed to be at least 15–30 mls (24–48 km) south of Caen. During the following night, the German defences north of Caen were reinforced by elements of the 12 *Waffen-SS Panzer Division 'Hitler Jugend'*—and from then on the British advance was checked every time an attempt was made to penetrate the German lines. Six weeks passed before the German troops could be forced out of their positions around Caen and then only after saturation bombing and relentless fighter-bomber attacks.

The plans, realities and tactics of the Normandy campaign are too complex to analyze here, but certain points must be made in order to understand the use of aircraft versus tanks during the Allied assault.

Already on D-Day the RP-armed Typhoons (sometimes known as 'Rockphoons') were instrumental in preventing German armour from reaching the front.

Among the German units ordered to be in readiness early on D-Day was the *Panzer Lehr Division* deployed in the Chartres-Le Mans-Orleans area. A new division, the *Panzer Lehr* was bigger than most but had never been in combat as a division. It received its movement orders at 1430 hrs and was to reach the area southwest of Caen by that evening. Objection by the divisional commander that such a move in daytime might result in heavy losses due to expected enemy air attacks were overruled, and *Panzer Lehr* set off that afternoon in several echelons. As dreaded by its commander, Lt Gen Fritz Bayerlein, who had seen Allied fighter-bombers in action in North Africa, the mixed armoured/motorised columns were spotted soon afterwards and attacked by relays of Typhoons from No. 123 Wing, RAF, with cannon, RPs and bombs. It was a textbook example of the well-practised 'shift' method: a squadron of Typhoons would attack till it had exhausted its ammunition and then be replaced by the next. Conditions for the attacking Typhoons were ideal: clear sky, no *Luftwaffe* fighters to worry about and weak and uncoordinated light Flak defences.

It was the first time the 60 lb (27 kg) RPs were used against such targets in action in large numbers, and the repeated Typhoon attacks had an almost traumatic effect on the largely inexperienced personnel of the *Panzer Lehr*. Not only that, the shock was so great that the troops never even made a real effort to defend themselves. Only the darkness brought some relief to the Germans, but the summer nights were short and the chaos created by the foregoing fighter-bomber attacks took time to sort out.

On that vital first day only 36 *Luftwaffe* aircraft were logged over the beachheads but none in support of their own armour.

It was not until D+2 that *Luftflotte* 3 began to receive any reinforcements, but the planned transfer of some 600 fighters from the Reich defence, Eastern Front and reserves soon became chaotic.

Under these conditions the lessons for the commanders of German armoured forces were clear, if not new: lacking any air cover, or sufficiently strong light Flak defences, it was suicidal to move in daytime. Movement by night of course was slower and tired out the troops before battle, but it could not be helped. And even the short nights were no longer a safe haven; the use of heavy RAF night bombers in a tactical role began on the night of 6/7 June when towns like Argentan were bombed into rubble to delay the movement of German armour.

Early in the morning of 7 June the PzKw IV detachment of *Panzer Lehr* was caught by Typhoons while refuelling in the woods north of Alençon. Despite careful camouflage the tanks were spotted from the air and attacked in waves. On that day, all RAF 83 and 84 Group squadrons were in action over Normandy attacking German armour and other important targets and a total of 17 Typhoons were shot down, all by Flak.

As is usual in such situations, the initial claims and damage reports were somewhat exaggerated, but the actual losses were serious nonetheless. The *Panzer Lehr* had lost five PzKw IVs, 84 self-propelled guns, armoured personnel carriers and half-tracks, 40 fuel tankers and about 90 other vehicles before it even got into action. Of much greater importance to the outcome of the battle at that crucial stage was the lost time which could no longer be made good.

This 'sacrificial march' of the only full-strength German Panzer division in Normandy at that time, as well as other Typhoon attacks on tanks of the 21 *Panzer* and 12 *SS Panzer Divisionen* during the first two days of the battle, resulted in some obvious as well as make-shift measures.

Orders were issued instructing all drivers to increase the distance between individual vehicles when on the move in daytime, with reminders about camouflage and the use of all

to be continued to page 58

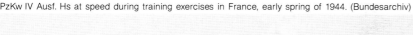
PzKw IV Ausf. Hs at speed during training exercises in France, early spring of 1944. (Bundesarchiv)

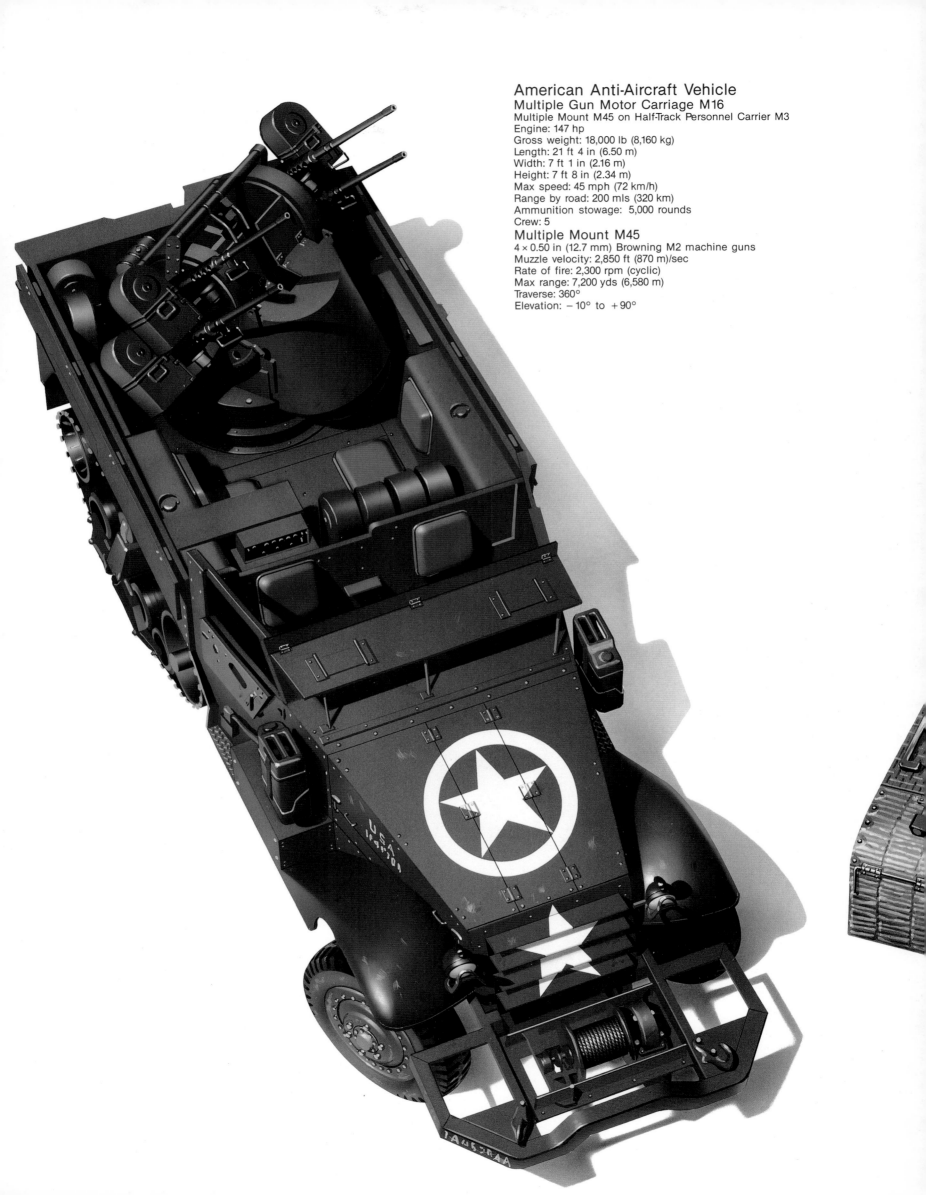

American Anti-Aircraft Vehicle
Multiple Gun Motor Carriage M16
Multiple Mount M45 on Half-Track Personnel Carrier M3
Engine: 147 hp
Gross weight: 18,000 lb (8,160 kg)
Length: 21 ft 4 in (6.50 m)
Width: 7 ft 1 in (2.16 m)
Height: 7 ft 8 in (2.34 m)
Max speed: 45 mph (72 km/h)
Range by road: 200 mls (320 km)
Ammunition stowage: 5,000 rounds
Crew: 5
Multiple Mount M45
4 × 0.50 in (12.7 mm) Browning M2 machine guns
Muzzle velocity: 2,850 ft (870 m)/sec
Rate of fire: 2,300 rpm (cyclic)
Max range: 7,200 yds (6,580 m)
Traverse: 360°
Elevation: −10° to +90°

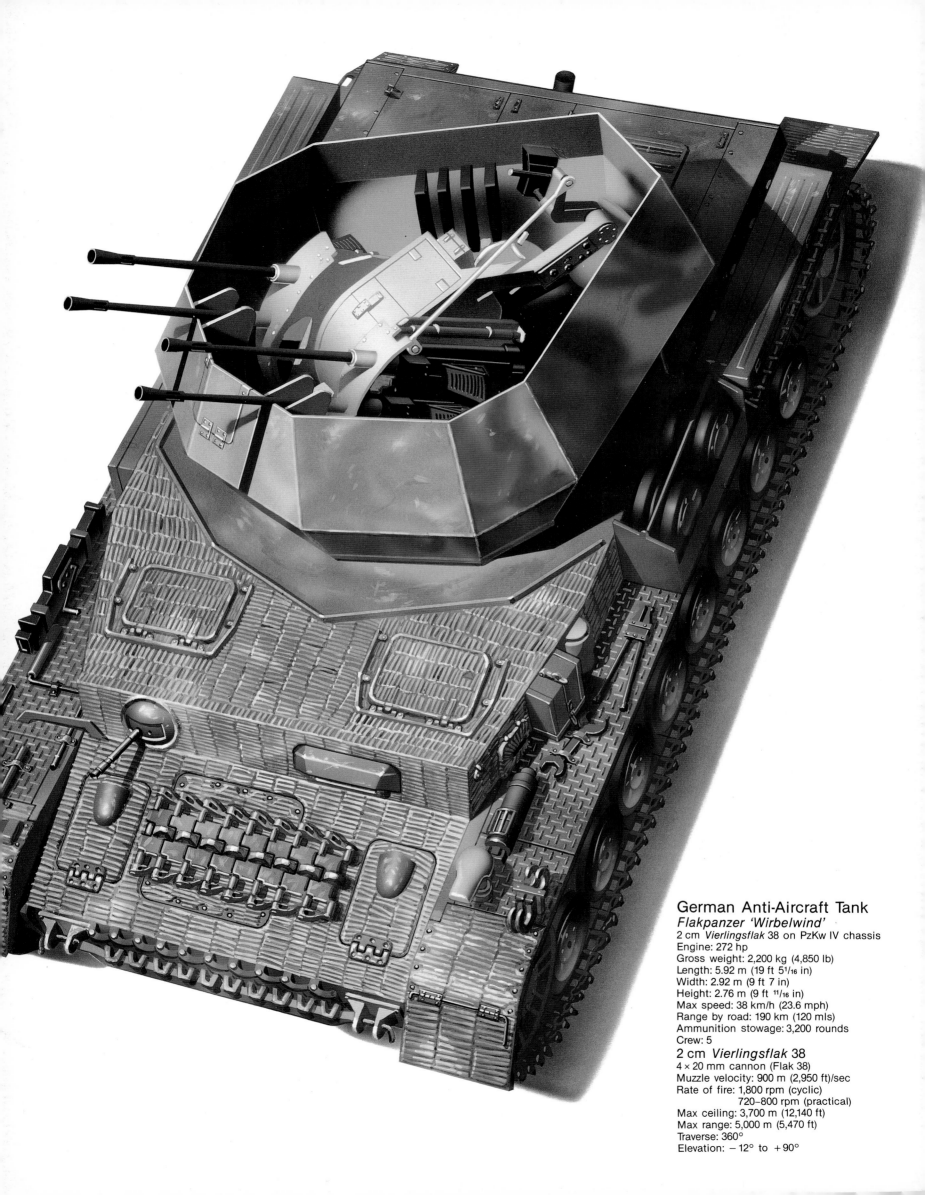

German Anti-Aircraft Tank
Flakpanzer 'Wirbelwind'
2 cm *Vierlingsflak* 38 on PzKw IV chassis
Engine: 272 hp
Gross weight: 2,200 kg (4,850 lb)
Length: 5.92 m (19 ft 5¹/₁₆ in)
Width: 2.92 m (9 ft 7 in)
Height: 2.76 m (9 ft ¹¹/₁₆ in)
Max speed: 38 km/h (23.6 mph)
Range by road: 190 km (120 mls)
Ammunition stowage: 3,200 rounds
Crew: 5

2 cm *Vierlingsflak* 38
4 × 20 mm cannon (Flak 38)
Muzzle velocity: 900 m (2,950 ft)/sec
Rate of fire: 1,800 rpm (cyclic)
720–800 rpm (practical)
Max ceiling: 3,700 m (12,140 ft)
Max range: 5,000 m (5,470 ft)
Traverse: 360°
Elevation: −12° to +90°

Known as 'nozhnitsi' (scissors), this Soviet *Shturmovik* attack method was most effective against extended or spaced-out columns of German armor or moto-mechanised troops and, as a rule, was carried out by pairs of Il-2 assaulters. Apart from ensuring protection against anti-aircraft fire, this tactic also enabled the *Shturmoviks* to take up advantageous positions to ward off attacks by intercepting enemy fighters.

Technical data contained here reflects aircraft shown on the inside of this gate-fo

Hawker Hurricane Mk IID
Power unit
Rolls-Royce Merlin XXII 12-cylinder liquid-cooled engine: 1,460 hp for take-off
Dimensions
Span: 40 ft 0 in (12.19 m)
Length, tail up: 32 ft 3 in (9.83 m)
Height, tail down: 10 ft 5 in (3.17 m)
Wing area: 247.5 sq ft (23.0 m²)
Weights
Empty: 5,550 lb (2,520 kg)
Gross: 7,850 lb (3,560 kg)
Performance
Max speed: approx. 300 mph (480 km/h) at sea level,
322 mph (518 km/h) at 22,000 ft (6,710 m)
Initial rate of climb: 1,613 ft (492 m)/min
Service ceiling: 32,100 ft (9,780 m)
Normal range: 420 mls (680 km)
Armament
2 × 40 mm 'S' cannon with 15 rpg
2 × 7.7 mm machine guns for sighting purposes

Republic P-47D-27-RE Thunderbolt
Power unit
Pratt & Whitney R-2800-59: 2,000 hp for take-off
2,430 hp in War Emergency Power
Dimensions
Span: 40 ft 9⁵/₁₆ in (12.43 m)
Length, tail up: 36 ft 1³/₄ in (11.02 m)
Height, tail down: 14 ft 8¹/₁₆ in (4.47 m)
Wing area: 300 sq ft (27.87 m²)
Weights
Empty: 10,000 lb (4,540 kg)
Gross: 14,500 lb (6,580 kg)
Performance
Max speed: 423 mph (681 km/h) at 30,000 ft (9,140 m)
Time to climb to 15,000 ft (4,570 m): 6.2 min
Service ceiling: 42,000 ft (12,800 m)
Normal range: 590 mls (950 km) at 25,000 ft (7,620 m)
Armament
6–8 × 12.7 mm machine guns with 267–425 rpg
6 × 4.5 in (114.3 mm) M10 rocket projectiles
Max bomb load: 2,500 lb (1,134 kg)

Ilyushin Il-2m3
Power unit
Mikulin AM-38F 12-cylinder liquid-cooled engine: 1,750 hp for take-off, 1,575 hp at 750 m (2,460 ft)
Dimensions
Span: 14.60 m (47 ft 10¹³/₁₆ in)
Length: 11.65 m (38 ft 2¹¹/₁₆ in)
Height: 3.40 m (11 ft 1⁷/₈ in)
Wing area: 38.5 m² (414.4 sq ft)
Weights
Empty: 4,525 kg (9,976 lb)
Gross: 6,160 kg (13,580 lb)
Performance
Max speed: 372 km/h (231 mph) at sea level
404 km/h (251 mph) at 1,500 m (4,920 ft)
Time to climb to 5,500 m (18,050 ft): 20min
Service ceiling: 6,500 m (21,330 ft)
Range with full ordnance: 765 km (475 mls) at 280 km/h (174 mph)
Armament
Fixed forward-firing: 2 × 23 mm VYa cannon with 150 rpg
2 × 7.62 mm ShKAS machine guns with 750 rpg
Flexible mounted aft-firing:
1 × 12.7 mm UBT machine gun with 150 rpg
8 × 82 mm RS-82 or 4 × 132 mm RS-132 rocket projectiles
2 × 250 kg (551 lb) bombs or
4 × 100 kg (220 lb) bombs
Crew
2

Hawker Typhoon Mk IB
Power unit
Napier Sabre IIA 24-cylinder liquid-cooled engine: 2,180 hp for take-off, 1,830 hp at 11,500 ft (3,510 m)
Dimensions
Span: 41 ft 7 in (12.67 m)
Length, tail up: 31 ft 11 in (9.73 m)
Height, tail down: 14 ft 10 in (4.52 m)
Wing area: 249 sq ft (23.13 m²)
Weights
Empty: 8,800 lb (3,990 kg)
Gross: 11,300 lb (5,130 kg)

Performance
Max speed: 405 mph (652 km/h) at 18,000 ft (5,490 m)
Time to climb to 15,000 ft (4,570 m): 6.2 min
Service ceiling: 34,000 ft (10,360 m)
Range with two 1,000 lb (454 kg) bombs: 1,000 mls (1,610 km)
Armament
4 × 20 mm Hispano Mk II cannon with 140 rpg
8 × 60 lb HE rocket projectiles or 2 × 1,000 lb (454 kg) bombs

Junkers Ju88P-1
Power unit
2 × Junkers Jumo 211J 12-cylinder liquid-cooled engines: 1,340 hp for take-off
Dimensions
Span: 20.08 m (65 ft 10⁹/₁₆ in)
Length without cannon, tail up: 14.96 m (49 ft 1 in)
Height, tail up: 5.07 m (16 ft 7⁵/₈ in)
Wing area: 54.7 m² (588.8 sq ft)
Weight
Gross: 11,070 kg (24,400 lb)
Performance
Max speed: 393 km/h (244 mph)
Armament
1 × 75 mm BK 7.5 (PaK 40) cannon with 12 rounds
1 × 7.92 mm MG 81 machine gun for sighting purposes
2 × flexible mounting MG 81Z installations (twin 7.92 mm MG 81 machine guns each) for air-defence
Crew
3

Henschel Hs129B-1/R1
Power unit
2 × Gnôme-Rhône 14M 4/5 14-cylinder air-cooled engines: 700 hp for take-off, 680 hp at 4,000 m (13,120 ft)
Dimensions
Span: 14.20 m (46 ft 7¹/₁₆ in)
Length, tail up: 9.75 m (31 ft 11⁷/₈ in)
Height, tail down: 3.25 m (10 ft 8 in)
Wing area: 29.0 m² (312.2 sq ft)
Weights (B-1/R2)
Empty equipped: 4,197 kg (9,253 lb)
Gross: 5,100 kg (11,240 lb)
Performance
Max speed: 407 km/h (253 mph) at 3,830 m (12,570 ft)
Time to climb to 3,000 m (9,840 ft): 7 min
Service ceiling: 9,000 m (29,530 ft)
Normal range: 560 km (350 mls)
Armament
2 × 20 mm MG151/20 cannon with 125 rpg
2 × 7.92 mm MG17 machine gun with 500 rpg
4 × 50 kg (110 lb) or 1 × 250 kg (551 lb) and 2 × 50 kg (110 lb) bombs

Junkers Ju87G-1
Power unit
Junkers Jumo 211J-1 12-cylinder liquid-cooled engine: 1,400 hp for take-off
Dimensions
Span: 15.00 m (49 ft 2⁵/₁₆ in)
Length, tail up: 11.50 m (37 ft 8³/₄ in)
Height, tail down: 3.90 m (12 ft 9½ in)
Wing area: 33.6 m² (361.7 sq ft)
Performance
Max speed: 260-270 km/h (160-170 mph) at low altitude
Armament
2 × 37 mm BK3.7 (Flak 18) cannon with 12 rpg
Crew
2

T-34-85 Model 1944
Engine
1 × V-2-34 12-cylinder diesel, 500 hp
Weight and dimensions
Combat weight: 32,000 kg (70,550 lb)
Length, overall: 8.15 m (26 ft 8⁷/₈ in)
Length, excluding gun: 6.00 m (19 ft 8¼ in)
Width, overall: 3.00 m (9 ft 10¹/₈ in)
Height: 2.72 m (8 ft 11¹/₁₆ in)
Armor
20-90 mm
Performance
Max speed by road: 55 km/h (34.2 mph)
Max speed across country: 40 km/h (24.9 mph)
Range by road: 300 km (186 mls)
Range across country: 210 km (130 mls)

Armament
1 × 85 mm ZiS S-53 Model 1944 L/54.6 gun with 60 rounds
2 × 7.62 mm DTM machine guns with 1,920 rounds in all
Without anti-aircraft machine gun
Crew
5

Medium Tank M4 (British name: Sherman I)
Engine
1 × Continental R-975 C1 nine-cylinder petrol, 400 hp
Weight and dimensions
Combat weight: 66,900 lb (30,350 kg)
Length: 19 ft 4 in (5.89 m)
Width, overall: 8 ft 7 in (2.62 m)
Height: 9 ft (2.74 m)
Armor
½–3½ in (13–89 mm)
Performance
Max speed by road: 24 mph (39 km/h)
Max speed across country: approx. 15 mph (24 km/h)
Range by road: approx. 120 mls (193 km)
Armament
1 × 75 mm M3 L/37.5 gun with 97 rounds
2 × 7.62 mm M1919A4 machine guns with 4,750 rounds in all
1 × 12.7 mm M2 anti-aircraft machine gun with 300 rounds
Crew
5

Cruiser Tank Mk VIA, Crusader III
Engine
1 × Nuffield Liberty 12-cylinder petrol, 340 hp
Weight and dimensions
Combat weight: 42,560 lb (19,305 kg)
Length: 19 ft 8 in (5.99 m)
Width, overall: 9 ft 1 in (2.77 m)
Height: 7 ft 4 in (2.24 m)
Armor
7–49 mm
Performance
Max speed by road: 27 mph (43 km/h)
Max speed across country: approx. 15 mph (24 km/h)
Range by road: 100 mls (160 km)
Armament
1 × 2 pounder (40 mm) L/50 gun with 110 rounds
2 × Besa 7.92 mm machine guns with 4,500 rounds in all
Without anti-aircraft machine gun
Crew
5

IS-2m (IS stands for Iosef Stalin)
Engine
1 × V-2-IS (V2K) 12-cylinder diesel, 513 hp
Weight and dimensions
Combat weight: 46,000 kg (101,410 lb)
Length, overall: 9.60 m (31 ft 6 in)
Length, excluding gun: 6.63 m (21 ft 9 in)
Width, overall: 3.12 m (10 ft 2¹³/₁₆ in)
Height: 2.71 m (8 ft 10¹¹/₁₆ in)
Armor
19–120 mm
Performance
Max speed by road: 37 km/h (23 mph)
Max speed across country: 20 km/h (12.4 mph)
Range by road: approx. 240 km (150 mls)
Range across country: approx. 200 km (124 mls)
Armament
1 × 122 mm D-25 Model 1943 L/43 gun with 28 rounds
3 × 7.62 mm DT machine guns with 2,330 rounds in all
1 × 12.7 mm DShK anti-aircraft machine gun with 945 rounds
Crew
4

Light Tank M24 Chaffee
Engine
2 × Cadillac 44T24 eight-cylinder petrol, 110 hp each
Weight and dimensions
Combat weight: 40,500 lb (18,370 kg)
Length, overall: 18 ft (5.49 m)
Length, excluding gun: 16 ft 4½ in (4.99 m)
Width, overall: 9 ft 8 in (2.95 m)
Height: 8 ft 1½ in (2.47 m)
Armor
9–44 mm
Performance
Max speed by road: 35 mph (56 km/h)

Max speed across country: approx. 25 mph (40 km/h)
Range by road: 100 mls (160 km)
Armament
1 × 75 mm M5 gun with 48 rounds
2 × 7.62 mm M1919A4 machine guns with 3,750 rounds in all
1 × 12.7 mm anti-aircraft machine gun with 440 rounds
Crew
4–5

Infantry Tank Mk III, Valentine V
Engine
1 × GMC six-cylinder diesel, 138 hp
Weight and dimensions
Combat weight: 39,000 lb (17,690 kg)
Length, excluding gun: 17 ft 9 in (5.41 m)
Width, overall: 8 ft 7½ in (2.63 m)
Height: 7 ft 5½ in (2.27 m)
Armor
8–65 mm
Performance
Max speed by road: 15 mph (24 km/h)
Max speed across country: approx. 8 mph (13 km/h)
Range by road: 90 mls (145 km)
Armament
1 × 2 pounder (40 mm) L/50 gun with 79 rounds
1 × Besa 7.92 mm machine gun with 3,150 rounds
Without anti-aircraft machine gun
Crew
4

Panzerkampfwagen III Ausf. J
Engine
1 × Maybach HL 120 TRM 12-cylinder petrol, 300 hp
Weight and dimensions
Combat weight: 22,300 kg (13,860 lb)
Length: 5.69 m (18 ft 8 in)
Width, overall: 2.95 m (9 ft 8¹/₈ in)
Height: 2.50 m (8 ft 2⁷/₁₆ in)
Armor
10–70 mm
Performance
Max speed by road: 40 km/h (24.9 mph)
Max speed across country: 19 km/h (11.8 mph)
Range by road: 175 km (109 mls)
Range across country: 100 km (62 mls)
Armament
1 × 5 cm KwK L/42 gun with 99 rounds
2 × 7.92 mm MG 34 machine guns with 2,000 rounds in all
Without anti-aircraft machine gun
Crew
5

Panzerkampfwagen IV Ausf. H
Engine
1 × Maybach HL 120 TRM 12-cylinder petrol, 300 hp
Weight and dimensions
Combat weight: 25,000 kg (55,110 lb)
Length, overall: 7.02 m (23 ft ³/₈ in)
Length, excluding gun: 5.89 m (19 ft 3⁷/₈ in)
Width, overall: 3.29 m (10 ft 9⁹/₁₆ in)
Height: 2.68 m (8 ft 9¹/₈ in)
Armor
5–85 mm
Performance
Max speed by road: 38 km/h (23.6 mph)
Max speed across country: 16 km/h (9.9 mph)
Range by road: 200 mls (124 mls)
Range across country: 130 km (81 mls)
Armament
1 × 7.5 cm KwK 40 L/48 gun with 87 rounds
2 × 7.92 mm MG 34 machine guns with 3,150 rounds in all
Some with 1 × 7.92 mm MG 34 anti-aircraft machine gun
Crew
5

Panzerkampfwagen V Panther Ausf. G
Engine
1 × Maybach HL 230 P 30 12-cylinder petrol, 700 hp
Weight and dimensions
Combat weight: 44,800 kg (98,770 lb)
Length, overall: 8.86 m (29 ft 1³/₁₆ in)
Length, excluding gun: 6.88 m (22 ft 6⁷/₈ in)
Width, overall: 3.43 m (11 ft 3 in)
Height: 3.00 m (9 ft 10¹/₈ in)

Armor
15–120 mm
Performance
Max speed by road: 46 km/h (28.6 mph)
Max speed across country: 25 km/h (15.5 mph)
Range by road: 200 km (124 mls)
Range across country: 100 km (62 mls)
Armament
1 × 7.5 cm KwK 42 L/70 gun with 81 rounds
2 × 7.92 mm MG 34 machine guns and 1 × 7.92 mm MG 34 anti-aircraft machine gun with 4,200 rounds in all
Crew
5

Medium Tank M 13/40
Engine
1 × Spa 8 TM 40 eight-cylinder diesel, 105 hp
Weight and dimensions
Combat weight: 14,200 kg (31,310 lb)
Length: 4.93 m (16 ft 2¹/₈ in)
Width, overall: 2.23 m (7 ft 3¹³/₁₆ in)
Height: 2.36 m (7 ft 8¹⁵/₁₆ in)
Armor
9–30 mm
Performance
Max speed by road: 33 km/h (20.5 mph)
Range by road: 200 km (124 mls)
Armament
1 × 47 mm gun with 104 rounds
2 × 8 mm machine guns with 3,048 rounds in all
Without anti-aircraft machine gun
Crew
4

Panzerkampfwagen VI Tiger Ausf. H (Tiger I Ausf. E)
Engine
1 × Maybach HL 210 P 45 12-cylinder petrol, 700 hp
Weight and dimensions
Combat weight: 56,900 kg (125,440 lb)
Length, overall: 8.24 m (27 ft 7/₁₆ in)
Length, excluding gun: 6.21 m (20 ft 4½ in)
Width, overall: 3.70 m (12 ft 1¹¹/₁₆ in)
Height: 2.88 m (9 ft 5³/₈ in)
Armor
26–100 mm
Performance
Max speed by road: 38 km/h (23.6 mph)
Max speed across country: 20 km/h (12.4 mph)
Range by road: 100 km (62 mls)
Range across country: 60 km (37 mls)
Armament
1 × 8.8 cm KwK 36 L/56 gun with 92 rounds
2 × 7.92 mm MG 34 machine guns with 4,500 rounds in all
Some with 1 × 7.92 mm MG 34 anti-aircraft machine gun
Crew
5

Panzerkampfwagen VI Tiger II (Königstiger) Ausf. B
Engine
1 × Maybach HL 240 P 45 12-cylinder petrol, 700 hp
Weight and dimensions
Max combat weight: 68,000 kg (149,910 lb)
Length, overall: 10.286 m (33 ft 9 in)
Length, excluding gun: 7.26 m (23 ft 9¹³/₁₆ in)
Width, overall: 3.755 m (12 ft 3¹³/₁₆ in)
Height: 3.09 m (10 ft 1¹¹/₁₆ in)
Armor
25–185 mm
Performance
Max speed by road: 40 km/h (24.9 mph)
Max speed across country: 17 km/h (10.6 mph)
Range by road: 120 km (75 mls)
Range across country: 80 km (50 mls)
Armament
1 × 8.8 cm KwK 43 L/71 gun with 84 rounds
2 × 7.92 mm MG 34 machine guns with 5,850 rounds
Some with 1 × 7.92 mm MG 34 anti-aircraft machine gun
Crew
5

Spitfire Mk IX and rocket-armed Typhoon Mk IB of 2 TAF in close support tasks on a Normandy landing ground a few days after D-Day. (Imperial War Museum)

available roadside cover. However, it soon became clear that this 'tactic' did not make much difference; there were far too many eyes in the sky on the lookout for just such targets, especially armour. Out of necessity some tanks had to move in daytime, so another 'innovation' was introduced in many German armoured units within a week of the Allied invasion—the lookout. A crew member of each tank on the move would sit behind the turret and scan the skies for the dreaded rocket-armed Typhoons. A last-minute warning was better than none at all!

Unfortunately the German armoured formations generally persisted in using roads instead of moving cross-country, thus considerably easing the task of Allied reconnaissance. This false economy of saving fuel and wear and tear of the tracks was to cost the Panzer divisions dear.

Due to the rail links destroyed by Allied pre-invasion bombing and the Allied aerial superiority in general, five of the remaining six Panzer divisions available to stem the invasion got involved in fighting only gradually, while another was not transferred from southern France until two months later. A point worth mentioning is that all these moves were detected and followed by Ultra, and the Allied commanders in Normandy informed accordingly. And yet despite the availability of numerous fighter-bombers armed with RPs and bombs, not to mention tactical bombers, the backbone of these German armoured formations remained intact, if progressively weakened, until August 1944.

During the first month after D-Day several attempts were made by the British troops to take Caen and the high ground behind it, but all were unsuccessful.

Basic Typhoon tactics while attacking armoured or mixed motorised columns on the move were also evolved during the first week in Normandy; every effort was made to block the front and rear of the column on the road before concentrating on the rest. The German observers also noted certain similarities in approach and attack methods, as well as the high proportion of 'wide' RPs that landed far from their presumed targets. The following cannon-fire straffing attacks were far more accurate, if less dangerous to armoured vehicles.

Examination of the shot-down Typhoons revealed another interesting fact: the attacks were invariably led by

formation commanders, with 'green' pilots bringing up the rear. The results were twofold: from then on, German ground defences concentrated more than ever on the leading aircraft, and the turnover of Typhoon squadron and flight leaders began to increase.

These points were also noted by RAF command who were well aware that many Typhoon pilots had received only superficial training in the use of RPs.

A new problem faced some Typhoon squadrons as soon as they began operating from advanced landing fields in Normandy. The steel mesh tracking did not prevent sand spilling up from the hurriedly bulldozed strips—and the local dust contained a proportion of hard silicone that could ruin their sensitive Napier Sabre sleeve-valve engines in less then ten hours of flying time. This led to the hurried design and provision of special sand dust filters to all Typhoons operating from levelled sandy strips, with some associated loss of serviceability.

In that period there were many more Typhoon attacks on German armour concentrating against the British sector, but only a small proportion of the German losses due to air attacks can now be verified.

For instance, from 6 June to 6 July 1944 inclusive the Typhoons of 124 Wing, 2 TAF (181, 182 and 247 Squadrons) participated in a variety of close support tasks. Of them, only seven operations were specifically against German armour. However, one of them was a 'special strike', as related below.

Flying from Hurn, north of Bournemouth, 124 Wing began its anti-tank activities on 7 June when all three Typhoon squadrons took off in rotation to attack German armour and other vehicles southwest of Caen, the last sortie landing at 2245 hrs. The same hectic pace continued on the following day, the first Typhoons taking off as early as 0432 hrs and rotation attacks continuing all day long. This time the targets were German tanks and other vehicles southeast of Caen and at Norrey-en-Bessin. Total claims: five tanks and one armoured car destroyed; one Typhoon was hit by Flak but managed to force-land behind the British lines. On 9 June bad weather precluded all air operations, while on the following day all three Typhoon squadrons of 124 Wing carried out various ground support tasks south/southwest of Caen. One, which qualified for the 'special strike' classification, developed from intelligence obtained by Ultra and involved a precision rocket attack on the mobile HQ of *Panzergruppe West*, which was practically annihilated by it.

The balance sheet of 124 Wing for those first 30 days over Normandy shows just 12 tanks and one armoured car destroyed, plus another four tanks damaged, at the cost of 11 Typhoons lost (six to enemy action) and one damaged. The number of RPs fired during these anti-tank operations is not known but could not have been less than 3,700, averaging out at about 308 RPs per tank confirmed destroyed—an enormous expenditure for the results achieved. This can be taken as representative of the other RP Typhoon wings at that time.

Due to the limited depth of the British sector the advanced landing grounds were often just a few kms from the front lines. In one notable case the Typhoons of 123 Wing operated from an advanced landing ground that was bulldozed over several mass graves of German dead and covered by SMT (Steel Mesh Tracking). As quick turn-around and combat readiness of the available Typhoons was an important factor, the planned speedy capture of the good airfield country beyond Caen was vital, but it was to remain firmly in German hands for nearly two months after D-Day.

Although a large number of German tanks and other armoured fighting vehicles had been hit and many destroyed by RP-armed Typhoons, British and American fighter-bombers, anti-tank guns and other weapons during the three weeks since D-Day, the German tank recovery service was generally very efficient, and only the complete write-offs remained on the battlefield. For that reason, the claims of early 'tank busting' sorties could seldom be substantiated, unless the target was obviously wrecked.

The fact remained that of the two most feared German battlefield weapons the Allies had practically eliminated the *Luftwaffe*, but despite overwhelming superiority in the air and on the ground the Panzer divisions, even when badly mauled, remained a force to be reckoned with. By late June 1944 practically whatever German armour was available in the West was concentrated against the British-Canadian sector.

Thanks to Ultra, the first major British offensive to break the deadlock, code named Epsom, was planned by General Montgomery with full knowledge of all German dispositions. It was to be carried out by two full corps with some 600 tanks, supported by 700 guns and every available squadron of RP-armed Typhoons, with other aircraft on call. The intention was to smash through the German lines and thrust inland beyond the crossings of the Odon and Orne rivers into the open 'tank country'. The offensive began on 23 June as planned but soon ran into determined German resistance, bolstered by small groups of tanks, and stalled. By 1 July it was all over.

During the next two days bad weather stopped all flying. Afterwards, apart from some local actions, there was stalemate in Normandy until 18 July when General Montgomery tried once more to move east of Caen, by then the proverbial thorn in his eye.

By the first week of July, according to Allied Intelligence (assisted by Ultra), the German forces were estimated to have 620 operational tanks of all types. About 500 were located opposite the British-Canadian sector, and the remainder deployed against the Americans. The Allied tank strength totalled 3,200, including about 1,000 light tanks. Unfortunately, the American share of this mass of armour was of no real consequence until a way could be found to get them past the marshlands and hedgerow-lined fields of the Cotentin peninsula. At the same time the lack of progress in the British sector was explained by the concentration of German armour, although the actual balance of strength did not really substantiate this claim.

By 8 July, the Second British Army outnumbered the German opposition by at least 2 : 1 in infantry and 4 : 1 in tanks, while the First British Army had a superiority of 3 : 2 in infantry and no less than 8 : 1 in tanks—not to mention the ever-present close air support.

Of course, right through this period the Allied fighter-bombers continued hunting their prime prey, the German tanks. The RP-armed Typhoons, now joined by the increasingly more aggressive American P-47 Thunderbolt squadrons, sought out German armour in their sector. As with the British 2 TAF, there were no specific American 'tank busting' tactical air force units. The priority of ground targets changed according to the combat situation, and no separate accounts of German armour attacked were kept. The only figures available for June are 14 tanks claimed destroyed by P-47s up to 18 June, and the estimated monthly total claimed by the Ninth AF fighters and bombers: 22 tanks destroyed, three probably destroyed and 21 damaged (as well as 1,288 motor vehicles destroyed, 114 probably destroyed and 469 damaged).

In the meantime, some interesting developments had taken place in the British sector.

A line of U.S. M4 tanks with 105 mm howitzers lays down a barrage from a French wheat field on 13 July 1944. (U.S. Army)

PzKw VI Tiger I Ausf. E with long-barrelled 88 mm gun in France, early summer 1944. (Bundesarchiv)

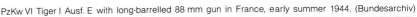

Carrying 108 U.S. gal (409 ltr) 'paper' fuel tanks, P-47Ds of the 366th FG, 9th AF, taxi on an airfield. (USAF)

On 5 July a representative of SASO (Senior Air Staff Officer) paid a visit to France to gather information on operational experiences with aircraft rockets.

For some reason, his visit was limited to a brief call at the headquarters of 83 Group, 2 TAF, at Creully so that the subsequent report does not really represent the views of all RP-armed Typhoon pilots, but the points discussed are nevertheless interesting:

1) There was no doubt that the 60 lb (27 kg) RP was effective against all types of armoured fighting vehicles and motor transport, as well as buildings and other ground targets, but one month after D-Day was deemed too early to evaluate results;

2) Pilots' claims were often found to be either exaggerated or understated and needed verification on the ground—not possible at that stage;

3) Effect on enemy morale was not certain, as only a few prisoners had been interrogated on that specific aspect. One German POW had stated that in his opinion the RP was the *least* effective form of air attack.

During the discussion that followed his visit it was proposed to increase the warhead size to be carried by Typhoons to 80–100 lb (36–45 kg) and possibly even 250 lb (113 kg). The decision to investigate the 100 lb RP warhead was seen as the best solution.

Another proposal recommended fitting whistles to the RPs to increase their noise in flight (shades of German Ju87 Stuka 'Trumpets of Jericho' of 1940–41!), and it was agreed to try this, provided accuracy was not affected.

The quick visit by the SASO representative also revealed some dissatisfaction with the RP; most of the 124 Wing Typhoon pilots preferred bombs to RPs, because they were trained as fighter pilots. After dropping its bombs, the Typhoon was free of all excess drag; after firing RPs, the aircraft still carried the launching rails and consequently experienced some loss in flight performance.

Other negative points included a certain carelessness in the storage and maintenance of these new weapons and a marked drop in accuracy in operational use. Some pilots were natural 'rocketeers', others acquired the skill after five or six sorties, but many younger and replacement pilots just fired them and got out. Due to the situation at the front it was not until autumn 1944 that Typhoon squadrons could be recalled to the UK in rotation for intensive seven to ten day RP training at Fairwood Common to improve their skill. Even with the train-

ing, however, the average squadron (18 to 20 pilots) performance seldom exceeded 50 percent of hits or near misses.

Goodwood is washed out

According to Overlord plans, by early July the British-American command had envisigned being in possession of the whole of Normandy and controlling 27 airfields in France, which would accomodate 62 squadrons. The reality was quite different; only about 20 percent of the projected area had been taken and the Allies had managed to establish only 17 advanced landing grounds able to support just 21 squadrons of their tactical air forces. In fact, by D+30 the British-Canadian forces only held a line originally planned for D+5.

As stated earlier, the British sector was by far the best for a breakout, and the failure to achieve any measurable progress was beginning to strain the Allied relations. Nobody realised this better than General Montgomery himself.

All this led to the planning of two almost identical breakouts, one in the American sector and the other in the British sector, both prepared with detailed knowledge of German dispositions and reserves supplied by Ultra, and both involving the use of strategic bombers to blow the initial gap in the German defences and destroy the opposing tanks and assault guns.

Preparations for both offensives were ready by mid-July when it was decided that the British attempt would be made first, the attack date originally being fixed at 17 July. Code named Goodwood, it was to be General Montgomery's biggest offensive in Normandy, carried out by three full-strength armoured divisions with attendant infantry of several

Two *Jagdpanzer* IVs, (SdKfz 162s) with heavy foliage camouflage against an Allied air attack in summer 1944. (Bundesarchiv)

Rocket-armed Typhoon Mk IBs of No. 198 Squadron, 123 Wing, depart for their ground support mission from the Plumetot airstrip in July 1944. (Imperial War Museum)

British corps. In armour alone, Montgomery had an easy 12 : 1 superiority.

However, despite the unique help rendered by Ultra the actual strength and depth of the German defences organised by the new commander of *Panzer Gruppe West*, General Heinrich Eberbach, were not fully appreciated. Worse, the German command had intercepted several signals and was aware of British preparations for an attack on 16 or 17 July.

Originally planned for 17 July, Operation Goodwood was launched on 18 July, an exceptionally clear and sunny day. Although it has little to do with 'tank busting' as such, it is of interest to recount the enormous effort invested by General Montgomery to neutralise the German armour before proceeding with his own tank attack—a clear proof of his respect for the fighting power of German Panzer units, no matter how decimated.

At 0530 hrs some 2,100 RAF and the Eighth AF heavy bombers began dropping an estimated 10,800 tons of bombs on the three selected target areas. A second bombing raid by medium bombers followed at 0700 hrs, and then another raid by B-24s at 0830 hrs dropped nearly 13,000 100 lb (45 kg) and more than 76,000 20 lb (9.1 kg) fragmentation bombs on and around the Bourguébus ridge. It was the heaviest tactical air bombardment of World War II. While the dust was still in the air, the combined artillery of three British corps and naval gunfire threw in another 250,000 shells of various calibres which—theoretically—had obliterated everything in that area.

But despite the enormous damage caused by this unprecedented bombardment (even 58-ton Tiger tanks were overturned by near misses) the destructive effect was limited. The bombardment had been too concentrated and too shallow; the German defences, even just behind the ploughed-up zone, were left relatively untouched, especially the deliberately scattered small sections of Tiger tanks and the 88 mm gun batteries. As a result, the British advance began to falter on the first day when the 11 Armoured Division lost 126 tanks and the Guards another 60.

The available RP-armed Typhoon squadrons had been operating in close support as soon as the smoke had cleared, but the German tanks were so well camouflaged that most of them escaped destruction. Strict instructions to tank commanders not to move or fire their guns when enemy aircraft were in the vicinity paid their dividends. Nevertheless, if the Typhoons had not interferred in the tank battle at Bourguébus ridge the British losses would have been more serious.

Perhaps the best proof of the success of German measures were the meagre results achieved by 124 Wing (181, 182 and 247 Sqns), 2 TAF. Operating at full 3-squadron strength all day long, 124 Wing could only claim two tanks and six other motor vehicles destroyed and one tank and eight other vehicles damaged, all for the loss of four RP Typhoons.

The British attack continued on 19 July but soon lost all impetus and ground to a halt again that evening. By then, British losses totalled more than 400 tanks, all to German ground defences, while according to some reports the Germans lost about 150 tanks. In both cases, more than half of these vehicles were later salvaged and repaired. Despite aerial superiority, Goodwood had not proved to be a 'racing certainty' for the Typhoons either.

The cobra strikes

The American attempt to break out of the difficult 'bocage' country and marshlands of their sector was code named Cobra, which after several postponements, finally struck on 25 July 1944.

The area selected was just west of St. Lô, where the Americans hoped to breach the German lines and aim for the general direction of the south coast of the Cotentin peninsula. There were no plans for any large-scale operations at that time, but events dictated otherwise.

Same as for the British Operation Goodwood, Cobra intended to use over 1,000 U.S. strategic bombers to blast a gap in the German defences and destroy the forward-deployed tanks and guns, preceded and followed by medium bombers and fighter-bombers.

The first recorded American 'tank busting' operation took place two weeks before Cobra. It happened on 11 July when the P-47Ds of the 366 FG attacked 32 German tanks of the *Panzer Lehr Division*, which had broken into the American lines towards the Vire canal. By dusk 20 PzKw V Panther and PzKw IV tanks had been knocked out, and the German attack stopped. Both sides learned a great deal from this encounter.

The German lines near St. Lô were held by units of the *Panzer Lehr* and what had remained of Fj Rgt 14 (parachute regiment). *Panzer Lehr* had arrived in the area in early July and had already been involved in some heavy fighting against the American troops. Altogether there were nine German infantry, two Panzer and one Panzergrenadier divisions facing the American troops along their sector—all of them already weakened by incessant fighting since D-Day.

The bombing area measured about 7,000 × 2,500 yds (6.4 × 2.3 km), just south of the Périers–Saint Lô road, held by some 5,000 *Panzer Lehr* soldiers and paratroops with perhaps 30 PzKw V Panther and 40 PzKw IV tanks (including reserves deployed further back). Like elsewhere in Normandy, the German troops were scattered among a series of strongpoints consisting of a nucleus of 2–3 tanks or self-propelled anti-tank guns with a group of infantry dug in around them.

The actual German losses due to the bombing and strafing tornado on 25 July could never be determined, although it is known that the primary target, German armour, was hardly touched: only five PzKw V Panther tanks were destroyed or burned out during the aerial onslaught, while all PzKw IVs survived—even if some of the crews were dazed.

The effect on the morale of the German troops was much more serious, and there were signs of panic and cases of insanity even among seasoned soldiers. It was one thing to face rocket-firing Typhoon 'tank busters' or fighter-bombers where one could at least manoeuvre, and quite another being helplessly cooped up inside a steel box exposed to 'carpet bombing' and then being hunted down by scores of enemy fighter-bombers. Furthermore, there was no sign of the *Luftwaffe*—already a dirty word among the German Normandy frontline soldiers, who could not know the true situation.

Within two days of the American attack the *Panzer Lehr* had ceased to exist as a combat formation. On 28 July the 1st U.S. Division of VIII Corps reached Coustances, and the German resistance was crumbling. The stalemate in Normandy had quite unexpectedly changed into a war of movement—and the Allied aircraft ruled the skies.

On 30 July, the 4 U.S. Armored Division, spearhead of VIII Corps commanded by General George Patton, reached Avranches, and on the following day gained a bridgehead across the Selune—the way was open to break into France proper. This was also realised by the German command, and the first attempt to counterattack was made by remnants of the 77 Infantry Division supported by 14 assault guns. Launched on 31 July, it made some good progress and the German troops managed to fight their way into Avranches, their target. However, by midday the skies cleared and the P-47s soon found their targets. In just one hour all 14 assault guns were knocked out and the German attack collapsed; there was nothing more to hold up the 4 U.S. Armored Division.

July was also the month the P-47Ds of the Ninth AF

Destroyed German SdKfz 231 armored car left amid the ruins of St. Lô, France, on 29 July 1944. (U.S. Army)

finally joined the rocket league.

Although trials with several types of aircraft anti-tank RPs had been carried out by American ordnance experts for some time, their accuracy was so unpredictable that P-47 pilots preferred steep dive bombing attacks on point targets, such as tanks. Only operational trials could really decide the issue and, on 17 July 1944, 12 P-47s of an IX TAC group used RPs in action for the first time, attacking the rail yard at Tiger-Quail and destroying and damaging a number of locomotives and wagons. German armour was next on the list.

On 26 July, the day American ground forces began to break through the German defences, the claims of individual P-47 flights added up to nine tanks destroyed (four by RPs, three by strafing, two by bombs) and three damaged (all by RPs). The strafed and destroyed tanks included two claimed as Tigers, none of which were anywhere near the area at that time—an understandable error; many late-production Pzkw IVs were described as 'Tigers' throughout the campaign.

In the same month some P-47Ds of the 513th Sqn, 406th FG, were modified to carry four high-velocity 5 in (127 mm) trackless RPs, two under each wing. Their first recorded use was against some German ammunition trucks at Gavray on 29 July. These rockets were in fact the forerunners of the later so well known 'Holy Moses' air-to-ground missiles and weighed 134 lb (61 kg) each.

Soon, pilots of 513 Sqn gained reputation as determined 'rocketeers' and their reports were carefully studied. One of their recommendations was the replacement of the standard 70 mm gunsight with a British 100 mm sight, which was easier to use.

In August 1944 the 406th FG and other units of the Ninth AF were supplied with the 4.5 in (114 mm) M-8 and M-10 one-piece ground attack/anti-tank rockets launched from triple 'bazooka'-type tubes, which were heartily disliked by the pilots. Their main drawbacks were the already noted inaccuracy, and the fact that their launching tubes could not be jettisoned, thus impairing the performance. On one later occasion, 513 Sqn was bounced by several Fw190s which shot down four of the rocket-carrying P-47Ds.

In August the Ninth AF P-47s were joined on ground support tasks by four Eighth AF P-47 formations, of which the 353 FG had pioneered the P-47 dive bombing technique.

Four sets of 4.5 in triple-tube RP installations with 60 M-8/M-10 rockets were provided for each of the four P-47 groups. The 56 FG and 353 FG immediately fitted trial installations to their P-47Ds, but the 78 FG and 356 FG were delayed by lack of the necessary tools. On some P-47Ds of 353 FG the total load carried consisted of two 500 lb (227 kg) bombs, six 4.5 in M-10 anti-tank rockets in two triple 'bazooka'-type clusters and a 165 U.S. gal (625 ltr) central drop tank.

All four Eighth AF P-47 groups participated on several ground attack operations in August and September 1944, but due to the additional drag of the rocket tubes all were later removed from most P-47s.

As a point of interest, by August 1944 all P-47Ds operating over the Western Front were marked with large white stars under both wings to 'convince' Allied anti-aircraft gunners they were not Fw190s.

However, despite the greater potential of aircraft rockets, bombs were to remain the favourite 'tank busting' weapon

Republic P-47D-5-RE of the 353rd FG about to receive a 500 lb (227 kg) HE bomb. (USAF)

of P-47 pilots until the end of hostilities in Europe.

The intensity of close support operations between 25–31 July 1944 is reflected in the official Ninth AF records, which list a total of 9,185 fighter-bomber sorties. Their ground claims included 384 tanks and 2,287 motor vehicles among 734 other targets destroyed or successfully attacked, for the loss of 78 aircraft shot down and 218 damaged. Of the above total, no less than 362 tanks and assault guns were claimed destroyed and 216 damaged (plus 1,337 other vehicles claimed destroyed and 280 damaged) by P-47s in the VII Corps sector alone.

The capture of Avranches by the First U.S. Army was not only the first strategic success of the Allied forces since D-Day, but was also to set off a completely unexpected sequence of events that within just two short weeks would doom the German armoured forces in France.

The first was a massive German armoured counter-attack at Avranches, ordered by Hitler. Only about 250 medium tanks could be deployed in time for that event, but the planned *Luftwaffe* support did not materialise.

Destined to be the most vital battle in Normandy, the outcome not only sealed the fate of the German Seventh Army but also the rest of the German forces in France. Even more important, it broke the back of the German tank forces in the West.

What none of the German soldiers or their command could even imagine was that Ultra had known about their attack almost from the very beginning, while still under preparation—and so did the American command.

In the early morning mist the attack continued, but soon the advancing German armour was stalled by determined American resistance, particularly by troops of the 30 U.S. Division holding Hill 317 which dominated the area.

When the morning fog began to lift, the German tanks were scattered deep in the Mortain-Avranches corridor, most of them on the main road for quicker advance. The goal was tantalisingly near, but their elation was short-lived. Several attempts were made to breach the American defences, but the resistance was too strong.

At midday, the last remains of the low clouds had disappeared—and the sky suddenly filled with dozens of Allied fighter-bombers. Within minutes, the blazing hot August day became a nightmare; the first great German tank slaughter on the Western Front had begun.

The battle of Mortain on 7 August was the first classic aircraft-versus-tank confrontation in the West since D-Day, with the German armour caught in the open.

Curiously, although the action took place in the American sector, it was the British 2 TAF that made by far the greatest contribution. Described dramatically as 'The Day of the Typhoon', this deadly contest raged from midday till dusk on that day. In the morning, there had been a request from the Ninth AF to the 2 TAF for assistance, which was promised as soon as the weather cleared. It was an emergency situation, and salvoes of 60 lb (27 kg) SAP RPs were far more effective anti-tank weapons than the bombs carried by the P-47s (as noted earlier, only a small number of P-47s were armed with anti-tank rockets).

This was a unique opportunity to show what the RP-armed Typhoons could really do against tanks in the open, all four 2 TAF wings based in Normandy were alerted. Before that, in between other targets, the Typhoons had faced mainly dug-in tanks forming the core of local German defences, with only the occasional Panzer caught hiding behind *bocage* boundaries. But this was different: a real confrontation!

By early August 1944 the Typhoon pilots of most wings had gained sufficient experience to make their rockets pay. The basic precepts were the minimum distance from the tanks—the 60 lb SAP needed about 2,000 m (2,200 yds) to reach maximum velocity for their warheads to punch through the tank armour—and 'hold steady when firing'—the slightest slip would scatter the rockets. The difficulty was judging the correct distance at attack speeds of 400–440 mph (645–710 km/h) in the usual 50–60° dive, especially when flying into concentrated Flak fire. The method, evolved by experience, was to fire the wing cannon while diving in an attempt to make some of the Flak crews take cover, jink the Typhoon out of its line of flight, and then steady it in the last moment before aiming and firing the RPs.

The crossroads of St. Barthélemy were the scene of the first rocket strike. The armoured column of the 2 *Panzer Division* had just reached it when the first Typhoons appeared. In the very first attack the two leading Tiger tanks were hit by several RPs and blown sideways across the road ditch, erupting into the first of many fireballs. Other Typhoons roared past the column at low level, searching for the next victims further back along the line.

Once again, the German armour had taken the easy way out and used a country road, which apart from flanking ditches and a few trees, has no protective cover anywhere. Not only that, having relied on the low cloud cover and morning mist, the German tanks and other vehicles were jammed together nose to tail and unable to scatter when the ground mist lifted—as it did very suddenly on 7 August. The Typhoons were on them before the tank drivers and the Flak gunners could react. The conditions and the target were ideal.

First rocket attacks were made on the leading and trailing vehicles to bring the column to a halt, and then to create maximum confusion, the Typhoons attacked along the whole length of the column.

The tactics employed by most Typhoon squadrons at Mortain were as follows:

a) The target was approached from about 5,000 ft (1,520 m) in two sections of four aircraft in 'finger-four' formation, the second section being slightly above and behind the first;

Natural metal finish P-47D Thunderbolts of the 36th FG, 23rd FS, 9th AF, return from ground attack duty. (USAF)

b) At the target the sections reformed into echelon port or starboard according to the direction of approach;

c) The attack was then made in a 30–40° dive from 4,000–5,000 ft (1,220–1,520 m), the RPs being fired by salvo or 'ripple' (two at the time) at about 1,000 ft (300 m);

d) The attack was broken off by a climbing turn to port or starboard.

Separate attacks were made on motor vehicles with wing guns in the same way, except that these attacks were broken off at very low altitude.

In practice, many Typhoons would fly along the column at about 5,000 ft, their pilots selecting their own targets before flicking over one by one to dive down, firing their cannon before releasing the RPs. They did not have to worry about fighter interception; they were assured of that.

However, once the initial surprise was over the German troops fought back with desperate urgency, multicoloured tracers reaching out to the jockeying Typhoons, and some losses were inevitable.

But what had happened to the promised *Luftwaffe* support for the Mortain counterattack?

Owing to the short notice most of the aircraft were simply not obtainable, but 300 fighters were organised—and all were intercepted by Allied fighters as soon as they had taken off from their bases around Paris. Once again, Ultra had warned the Allied command in good time to plan this interception some 200 km (125 mls) from the intended target. It paid off handsomely: not one of the 300 Bf109s and Fw190s reached the battle zone. The German tank crews and ground troops were left to fight for their lives on their own.

By the afternoon, the numerous columns of smoke streaming up from the doomed German column had grown into several greasy dark layers punctuated by explosions on the ground, but the anti-aircraft fire was also taking its toll. For some reason very few German tanks tried to disperse across the fields; instead, their crews fought back from their vehicles. As the day wore on, they started to run short of ammunition, while others simply left their tanks for the safety of the nearest ditch. But they stood their ground, even if most of the men had never experienced an air attack of this intensity.

This unique battle lasted several hours until, by late afternoon, the German attack was broken. Several P-47 groups of IX TAC were also involved from midday onwards, but mainly in dive bombing and strafing German armour and troops away from the roads, to avoid getting entangled with the Typhoons.

When the dusk came most of the German tanks had been knocked out, but within an hour of the last fighter-bombers leaving the scene German tank recovery teams were in

action to save what could be saved, and many valuable vehicles were towed away to safety. The remaining tanks and the Panzer-grenadiers held the ground they had taken, and plans were in hand to renew the attack on 9 August, but it was not to be. On 7 August, preceded by another massive aerial blow, fighting had suddenly erupted along the British-Canadian sector as well. At the same time, General Bradley had ordered Patton's XV Corps to swing north towards Alençon and Argentan, behind the German Seventh Army.

The foundations for the next and bloodiest aerial 'tank busting' operation in the West had been laid.

In hard facts and figures, the unique rocket-versus-tank battle at Mortain was waged between about 150 Typhoons and some 220 German tanks and other armoured fighting vehicles, as well as several hundred 'soft-skinned' motor vehicles. The RP-armed Typhoons flew a total of 1,014 sorties, firing more than 4,000 60 lb SAP RPs. Their pilots claimed 84 tanks destroyed and 55 damaged, plus another 112 vehicles hit or left burning. The cost added up to at least 14 Typhoons, but only three pilots were killed.

As fighting was still in progress, the claims could not be checked until about a week later. A total of 39 tanks and 58 other vehicles (or their remains) were examined. Of these, 24 tanks were found to be destroyed, ten damaged and five abandoned; 32 other vehicles were destroyed, 23 damaged and three abandoned.

In the number of tanks, this was only about 28 percent of the original claims, but there was clear evidence that many tanks had been salvaged.

An official RAF analysis of this battle pointed out that it was an exceptional encounter in several ways: an ideal target, with tanks and other vehicles nose to tail in close country; opposition was negligible; and the maximum effort was employed at a critical stage of the battle. Interrogation of the German prisoners taken after the encounter gave clear proof that the German tank crews were frightened of RPs. They were aware that in case of a direct hit their chances of survival were minimal. The demoralising effect of aircraft rockets was shown by the number of tanks and other vehicles abandoned which, according to POW statements, was much greater during the battle.

The available Ninth AF records of this German counterattack only lists operations beginning 8 August, the day after the initial assault. According to these records, between 8–14 August 1944, IX TAC flew 4,012 sorties over the battle zone, and the 532 sorties flown on 8 August resulted in claims of 47 German tanks and 122 other motor vehicles destroyed. Most of the other sorties were flown in direct ground support on a variety of other targets.

The American ground troops were effusive in their praise for the effectiveness of the RAF rocket attack. They admitted that had the German attack continued with the same determination as before the rocket strike they would have been unable to stop it. The seriousness of the situation was confirmed some time later by General Bradley, when he stated that 'Our defences were much thinner south of Mortain. Had the enemy sidestepped his Panzers by several thousand yards, he would have broken through to Avranches that very first day.'

But the Germans had no Ultra to keep them informed.

Falaise—the killing ground

The annihilation of the German tank force in the West happened two short weeks after the Mortain–Avranches attack as a result of several widely separated events taking place within a few days.

It began with the transfer of several German tank formations westwards to participate in that counterattack, and it was speeded up by the success of Allied fighter-bombers in stopping it. Having planned another breakout, General Montgomery then decided to capitalise on the American success of Cobra and advance the date of his attack to 7 August, using the opportunity to strike south when the German armour was weakened on his front. The goal was a little French town named Falaise, which would open the way into the rear of the German Seventh Army.

With the first light on 7 August, scores of RP-firing Typhoons appeared over the battlefield, attacking gun positions and other targets immediately behind the German lines, and neutralising all forward movement of reserves. But their main task was, as always, to seek out and destroy all German armour, either dug in or on the move.

By then, the German mechanised troops had learned to use some tricks to fool the Allied fighter-bombers, as revealed by an order issued on 4 August by 12 *Waffen-SS Panzer Division* 'HJ' to drivers of all vehicles who had to be on the move in daylight: 'If your vehicle is attacked by fighter-bombers, drop a smoke candle (*Rauchkörper*) close to the vehicle. When the pilot thinks he has hit the target he usually sheers off. Never drop the smoke candle before the first burst of fire, or the enemy will notice the trick...In future every vehicle is to be equipped with two smoke candles.'

The development and annihilation of the so-called 'Falaise pocket' is really a story of missed chances.

Once again, this is no place to describe or analyse the many stages of this battle; that has been done in dozens of other publications. However, some of the decisions made at that time will probably remain controversial forever. Likewise, no one will ever know the actual German losses either in men or material, because the battle was a confused and, by Western standards, unbelievable wholesale destruction of war material and merciless slaughter of men and panic-stricken horses—mostly from the air.

The eventual destruction of practically all remaining German armour in Normandy and most of the Seventh Army could have been avoided, or at least greatly minimised, if Hitler had not insisted on continuing preparations for another attack towards Avranches and the sea, in the forlorn hope of cutting the American supply lines. The writing was on the wall after Patton's ranks had turned north from Le Mans.

On 15 August came Operation Anvil-Dragoon, the landing of American-French forces in southern France, against

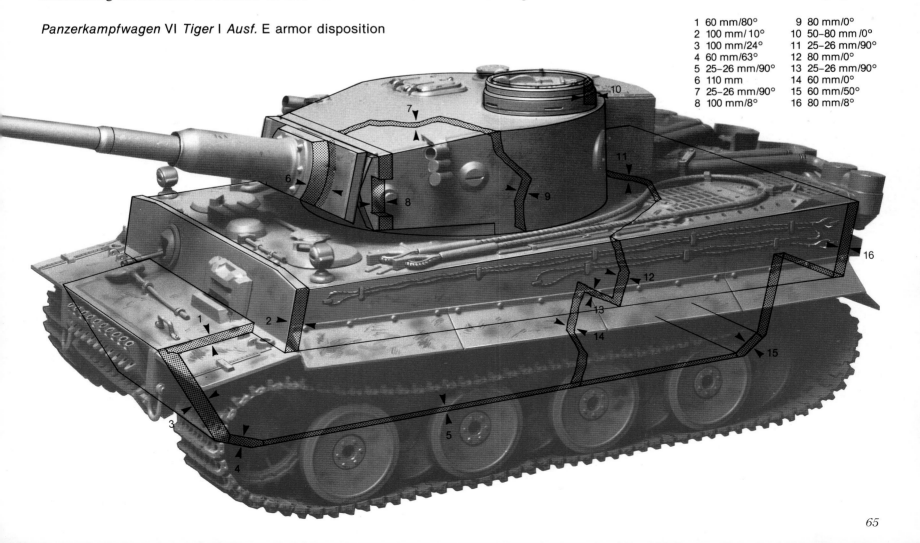

Panzerkampfwagen VI *Tiger* I *Ausf.* E armor disposition

1	60 mm/80°	9	80 mm/0°
2	100 mm/10°	10	50–80 mm /0°
3	100 mm/24°	11	25–26 mm/90°
4	60 mm/63°	12	80 mm/0°
5	25–26 mm/90°	13	25–26 mm/90°
6	110 mm	14	60 mm/0°
7	25–26 mm/90°	15	60 mm/50°
8	100 mm/8°	16	80 mm/8°

A No. 609 Squadron Typhoon Mk IB with eight 60 lb (27 kg) RPs takes off from an advanced airfield in France. (Imperial War Museum)

weak resistance. A day later, the Canadian 2 Division finally captured the ruins of Falaise, flattened by an RAF bombing raid on the night of 12/13 August. That still left a gap of almost 20 mls (32 km) to the nearest Allied forces (2 French Armoured Division), although a 'short hook' envelopment by VII U.S. Corps had already made contact with British forces east of Mortain.

Be as it may, what had started out as a bold enveloping operation with the price of some 150,000 German troops including eight or nine Panzer divisions, had degenerated into a gradually shrinking balloon squeezing out the German troops through its open end, which should have been closed several days ago. The big chance had been missed. This led to the first inter-Allied recriminations, which have not been resolved to this day.

One of the measures taken to speed up the operation at that time was an order to all Allied tactical air formations to intensify their attacks on the retreating German troops, the idea being to destroy as much as possible and stampede the rest— even if it was not so worded in the orders. With all that, tanks and other transport remained priority, as evidenced by combat reports of Allied air formations. Thus, on 13 August P-47s of IX TAC alone flew 649 sorties and claimed 106 armoured fighting vehicles and 570 motor vehicles. On that day, the German predilection for using roads for the movement of their armour, and sloppy camouflage, cost them six tanks in as many minutes. While operating near Carrouges, some 366 FG pilots spotted two trucks under trees on a road, then some more trees in the *middle* of the road. A closer look revealed some 30 fuel tankers in the area and at least six tanks refuelling from them. The 366 FG immediately attacked, strafing and bombing, with predictable results.

On the same day, the only American rocket-armed 'tank busting' unit, 513 Sqn of 406 FG (XIX TAC) successfully attacked four heavy and one light German tank, claiming all five destroyed. On 16 August the 2 TAF claimed three tanks destroyed and six damaged, plus 106 motor vehicles destroyed and 159 damaged; the Ninth AF score for that day was 30 tanks claimed destroyed and 18 damaged, plus 214 motor vehicles destroyed and 51 damaged.

However, from 17 August the Allied tactical air forces operating over the Falaise 'pocket' were given practically a free hand and the RAF RP-armed Typhoons in particular excelled in these destructive aerial assaults. The few roads were congested, and there was no escape from the bombs, shells and rockets. Many German tanks and other armoured fighting vehicles were simply abandoned or destroyed by their own crews for lack of

fuel, with their fuel tankers stuck somewhere on the congested roads, surrounded by other vehicles and dead or dying horses, the most tragic aspect of this battle.

By the evening of 17 August 1,471 sorties had been flown over the 'pocket', the pilots claiming 90 tanks and 1,100 motor vehicles destroyed. Of this total 124 (RP) Wing alone accounted for 26 tanks destroyed and 15 damaged, plus 194 motor vehicles destroyed and 120 damaged in 177 sorties, for the loss of five Typhoons (all to ground fire).

The last remaining gap was closed on Saturday, 19 August, by troops of the 1 Polish Armoured Division and 90 U.S. Division joining forces at Chambois. On that day, the Allied tactical air forces flew a series of concentrated rocket and strafing attacks on the German troops trapped in the 'pocket', and the confusion and slaughter were appalling.

The figures speak for themselves. According to official records, on 19 August the 2 TAF claimed 124 tanks destroyed and 96 damaged, plus 1,159 motor vehicles destroyed and 1,724 damaged. Of this total, 124 (RP) Wing claimed seven tanks destroyed and 14 damaged, as well as 75 motor vehicles destroyed and 72 damaged in 136 sorties, for the loss of four Typhoons (again, all to ground fire).

However, such intense and concentrated tactical air operations over a limited area also had their drawbacks: the congestion on the ground and in the air was such that an increasing number of air strikes were misdirected and caused Allied casualties.

With all that, nobody seems to have kept a tally of the casualties, and the same applies to the tanks and other war material destroyed or captured. The original claims were obviously exaggerated, but over 700 tanks and other armoured fighting vehicles were quoted as confirmed. The British No. 2 Operational Research Unit counted 187 tanks and self-propelled guns, 157 light armoured vehicles, 1,778 trucks, 669 smaller motor vehicles and 252 guns, mostly around the St. Lambert area, while the American (western) portion of the 'pocket' contained 220 tanks, 160 assault guns, over 5,000 vehicles and 700 pieces of ordnance.

There are no accurate German figures for their losses of armour at Falaise, but according to German estimates, from 6 June to the end of August 1944 the Army Group B lost 1,300 tanks, 500 assault guns, 20,000 motor vehicles of all kinds, 1,500 pieces of artillery and 3,000 anti-tank and anti-aircraft guns. As the tanks and assault guns were all usually classed as 'tanks' in Allied reports, this would add up to 1,800 tanks lost. Other German sources mention 2,100 tanks and assault guns. The total personnel losses in that period amounted to 450,000 men.

After Falaise, there were no large-scale aircraft-versus-tanks encounters on the Western Front, although the German tanks, assault guns and other armoured fighting vehicles remained priority targets till the end of hostilities.

From late August onwards, the Allied tactical air power was used against all kinds of targets of that nature, including armour wherever revealed. For example, the XIX TAC supporting Patton's TUSA alone claimed 466 tanks and other armoured fighting vehicles, and 4,058 motor vehicles destroyed in August 1944; its fighter-bombers flew 12,292 sorties and lost 114 aircraft.

Interestingly, the .50-cal (12.7 mm) API ammunition used by the P-47s could set on fire and destroy German armoured fighting vehicles if attacks were made at low altitudes from the rear, aiming for the engine compartment—exactly as noted by the *Luftwaffe* 'tank busters' on the Eastern Front a year previously.

In the period between 27 September and 16 December 1944 the three TACs of the Ninth AF alone claimed 688 German tanks and other armoured fighting vehicles destroyed and 496 damaged, plus 8,922 motor vehicles destroyed and 2,181 damaged. From 1 September to 30 November the P-47s of these three TACs flew 34,188 effective sorties against all kinds of ground targets, losing 274 aircraft. In the same period the British 2 TAF lost 121 Typhoons, which mostly attacked targets other than German armour.

Code named '*Wacht am Rhein*' (Watch on the Rhine), the Ardennes offensive was the first and only time Ultra failed to give an advance warning—mainly because of much stricter security—although there were other indications. It was also the last occasion in World War II that more than 500 German tanks were in action in the West at the same time.

On the morning of the German assault, 16 December, a thick fog and low clouds limited the Ninth AF activities to just 437 sorties, while the *Luftwaffe* managed to fly 150 ground support sorties. On 18 December the Ninth AF recorded its first 'tank busting' operation in the Ardennes. In bad weather, two volunteer F-6 (reconnaissance variant of P-51) pilots spotted a concentration of 60 German tanks near Stavelot and immediately contacted the IX TAC by radio. The following series of bombing attacks by four-plane sections of P-47s of 365 FG and 368 FG lasted until dusk at 1700 hrs, leaving 32 armoured fighting vehicles and 56 motor vehicles destroyed.

On the following four days the weather was extremely bad, but soon afterwards 406 FG made a name for itself while flying in support of the beleaguered Bastogne defenders. During the period 23–27 December it flew 81 missions (529 sorties), operating from dawn till dusk within a 10-mile (16 km) radius of the town, carrying out rocket attacks against all kinds of tactical targets. In these five days, 406 FG claimed 194 German tanks and other armoured fighting vehicles, 610 motor vehicles, 226 gun positions and many other local targets were destroyed or badly damaged. In the process they shot down or damaged 14 German aircraft—a truly commendable performance.

A day later the first German tanks began to run out of fuel, just when the Allied counterattacks were set in motion; their urgently needed petrol tankers were shot up by Ninth AF fighter-bombers way behind the lines. On 27 December it was all over.

During the period 16–27 December the Ninth AF TACs flew a total of 4,860 sorties against all kinds of ground targets. The recorded claims of their P-47 groups totalled 459 tanks and other armoured fighting vehicles and 1,356 motor vehicles destroyed or damaged.

During the same period the *Luftwaffe* achieved more than 1,600 sorties by day, but it is not known if any of these involved the use of airborne anti-tank weapons.

From the 'tank busting' point of view, the last few months of hostilities did not reveal anything new. No new Allied airborne anti-tank weapons were introduced in Europe; all 'tank hunting' remained the task of fighter-bombers armed with rockets, bombs and wing guns, depending on the target.

RP was overtaking the bomb as the most effective means of point-target destruction. By the end of hostilities in Europe the aircraft RP had been greatly improved and so were their launching methods. By late 1944 the much more accurate 'zero length' launchers had been tested on Typhoons, P-47s and Spitfires, although they did not become widely available in Europe. However, there were still no hard and fast rules regarding the tactics on how best to use the aircraft RPs against tanks and other armoured fighting vehicles. Some pilots preferred to fire them in a dive; others, to launch their RPs from a low-level inclined attack flight.

Apart from more constant burning, propellant accuracy of the RPs could only be improved by special sights and guidance mechanisms, but such advanced aircraft RPs remained in prototype stage when the hostilities ended in Europe. As for proper sights, the Typhoon pilots had nothing better than their standard Mk II reflector gunsight, often with diving angles marked on it by the pilot himself. A rocket sight had to allow for trajectory drop and wind effect, but such refinements did not appear until much later. As it was, the average error in range and trajectory estimation could be as high as 150 ft (50 m) at 1,200 yds (1,100 m) range. Even with accurate aiming by experienced pilots, however, some 20–30 percent of the RP warheads failed to explode.

Generally lacking fighter cover in 1944–45, the German tanks defended themselves as best as they could, from passive measures (more careful or misleading camouflage, all movement by night or under bad weather conditions) to more active means, such as being accompanied by mobile light anti-aircraft guns when on the move in daytime. This mobile protection was taken to its logical conclusions by combining

The latest type Panther, PzKw V Ausf. G, knocked out by American aircraft. Photographed near Ploy, France, on 14 October 1944. (U.S. Army)

A wreck of StuG III (SdKfz 142/1) Ausf. G destroyed by American P-47Ds outside Daleiden, Germany. February 1945. (U.S. Army)

Night ground attack version of Fw190G-2s fitted with 300 ltr (79 U.S. gal) drop tanks for long-range mission among the trees in Germany, early autumn of 1944. Note the flame-suppression exhaust nozzles. (Bundesarchiv)

multi-barrel light anti-aircraft guns with armour protection, mounted on PzKw III chassis like the *Wirbelwind* and similar developments.

Curiously, not much attention was paid to the turret-mounted anti-aircraft machine gun; although most German tanks could be fitted with one, very few ever carried it. No attempt was made to increase the calibre (and therefore effectiveness) of the turret-mounted machine gun, while practically all American tanks carried a .50-cal weapon on a universal mount.

Belatedly, a crash programme to evolve small guided anti-aircraft rockets to defend armoured formations and other vital targets was initiated in 1944, but none advanced beyond the experimental stage before the German capitulation.

That German armour and motor vehicles were priority targets all the way is clearly shown by figures tabulated by the Ninth AF during its campaigns in Europe. From 6 June 1944 to 8 May 1945, the three TACs under its control claimed no less than 4,509 tanks and other armoured fighting vehicles destroyed and 3,751 damaged, plus 53,811 motor vehicles destroyed and 22,546 damaged, for the loss of 1,374 P-47s.

Another yardstick is the number of aircraft RPs used. Being the preferred anti-tank and ground support weapon of the RAF, the 2 TAF records show 222,515 RPs (143,327 by the Typhoons of 83 Group alone) fired in combat, while the Ninth AF, whose fighter-bomber pilots put their trust in bombs and made only limited use of rockets, added another 13,783 fired (and 344 jettisoned) against armour vehicles and other ground targets.

Unfortunately no exact total figures are available for all 2 TAF Typhoon wings, but those of 124 Wing can be taken as representative. Between 6 June 1944 and 1 January 1945, its pilots claimed 115 German tanks and two armoured cars destroyed and 76 tanks and one armoured car damaged, plus 494 motor vehicles destroyed and 292 damaged. On the other hand, the Typhoon losses reflect the intensity of their ground support operations: from 6 June to the end of December 1944, 407 Typhoons (as against 953 P-47s), and from 1 January to 8 May 1945, another 163 Typhoons (421 P-47s). In looking at these figures one has to bear in mind that there were fewer Typhoons available for operations than P-47s, and therefore their loss rate was proportionally far more serious. There was no gradual decline of these losses until the last month of fighting; even in February 1945, just two months before the end, 150 P-47s and 57 Typhoons were lost.

The fact that the badly needed *Luftwaffe* close support/ground attack aircraft—not to mention the 'flying tank busters'—were conspicuously absent from Normandy (and, later, the Western Front in general) was due to several reasons, in addition to the Allied aerial superiority: lack of own fighter protection, increasingly better Allied ground defences and, as time went on, shortage of fuel and lack of sufficiently trained replacements. The experiences in Italy had shown this only too clearly already in spring 1944; SG 4 flying Fw190F close support fighter-bombers was losing on average 30–50 pilots per month. The brief appearance over the D-Day beaches of a few Hs129Bs from a training unit had no significance.

Later in the autumn of 1944 attempts were also made to attack Allied armour, motor vehicles, HQs and dumps at night by Ju87D-7 night attack bombers usually working in pairs, while NSGr 20 operated at night with Fw190G-2 fighter-bombers, but this was hardly 'tank busting'.

As noted earlier, the development of German air-to-ground rockets and particularly their use as anti-tank weapons lagged behind the Allies. When the 80 mm *Panzerblitz* Pb 1 anti-tank aircraft rockets finally became available in late autumn 1944, most of the limited number of Fw190F rocket-armed 'tank busters' were used on the Eastern Front. However, in December 1944 a detachment of such rocket-armed Fw190F-8 'tank busters' was also deployed in the West, and flew some sorties that month. Unfortunately no details of these operations have survived, but one Fw190F-8 armed with six Pb 1 rockets fitted under each of the two electrically-operated underwing projector rails was captured by British forces near Asch in Holland on 1 January 1945.

When the fighting ended in Europe no record seems to have been made of German tanks and other armoured fighting vehicles captured or found abandoned.

The once vaunted *Luftwaffe* however was more carefully recorded, and the RAF Disarmament Teams alone 'neutralised' 4,810 different types of German aircraft and 12,800 aero engines between December 1944 and December 1946. Among them were a small number of Ju87Gs and Hs129Bs, the only really dedicated 'tank busters' evolved during World War II, which never had a chance to show what they could do in the West.

The only survivor is the Ju87 now displayed in the Battle of Britain Museum at Hendon, near London; it is in fact a Ju87D-3/trop converted to G configuration with hard points for the BK 3.7 cannon and the original short-span wings.